THE
TOMATO
COOKBOOK

THE
TOMATO
COOKBOOK

Victoria Lloyd-Davies

a Salamander book

Published by Salamander Books Limited
LONDON

IN ASSOCIATION WITH
BRITISH TOMATO GROWERS

A SALAMANDER BOOK

Published by Salamander Books Ltd
129-137 York Way
London N7 9LG
United Kingdom

© Salamander Books Ltd, 1994

1 3 5 7 9 8 6 4 2

ISBN 0 86101 775 7

All correspondence concerning the content of this volume should be addressed to
Salamander Books Ltd.

CREDITS

COMMISSIONING EDITOR: *Will Steeds*
EDITOR: *Miranda Spicer*
DESIGN: *The Design Revolution, Brighton*
PHOTOGRAPHER: *Simon Butcher*
HOME ECONOMIST: *Wendy Dines*
STYLIST: *Marion Price*
COLOUR SEPARATION: *P & W Graphics Pte Ltd*

Printed in Singapore

ABOUT THE INGREDIENTS
When making any of the recipes in this book, you should follow either the metric or the
imperial measures, as these are not interchangeable.
As seasoning is a matter of personal taste, salt and pepper are not
necessarily listed in the ingredients.
Try to obtain the best quality fresh produce.

CONTENTS

AUTHOR'S INTRODUCTION

The fragrant smell of fresh garden tomatoes always reminds me of summer. Nothing can beat a sliced tomato salad sprinkled with a little chopped basil, a pinch of both caster sugar and ground black pepper and a drizzle of extra virgin olive oil. A glass of chilled white wine and some freshly baked crusty bread turns this simple dish into a summer meal. Second on my list of favourites is a freshly made tomato sandwich served with a cup of tea. Although the simplest dishes are often the best, so many can be cooked with this versatile vegetable.

My early adult summers were spent on the Adriatic coast of southern Italy. As I was the only 'trained cook' at my uncle's house, it was left to me to do most of the cooking. I remember the tomato–laden lorries winding their way over the mountains to Naples, and the boxes of warm plum tomatoes in the local village shops. I used them constantly; raw in salads at lunchtime and cooked in sauces with pasta, fish, poultry and meat in the evenings. I never weighed them. With the help of this constant supply of tomatoes I was able to turn very simple ideas into beautiful, rich red tasty dishes. The secret is not to be mean with tomatoes in cooking; use a plentiful supply.

More recently I have spent holidays in the Greek islands. I return with fond memories of going into taverna kitchens to choose our family meals and seeing roasting pans filled with enormous stuffed beef tomatoes. They are wonderful when they are freshly cooked and hot.

I have brought together a fund of tomato recipes for *The Tomato Cookbook*. Many are family favourites with ideas for special occasions. Fresh tomatoes dominate but some of my recipes feature sun-dried tomatoes to strengthen the flavour; others use convenient products such as canned tomatoes, purées and pastes. I have tried to include a large variety of recipes, ranging from attractive and enticing hot or cold starters to robust chutneys and pickles.

Today we see many varieties of tomatoes coming into our shops. The traditional round tomato is still the most popular but now there are many different sizes and flavours to choose from. The new cherry tomatoes are so sweet you can pop them into your mouth like sweets. Put a bowlful out with drinks alongside the traditional nibbles. Buy plenty of them as you will be refilling the bowl more than once! Look out for the yellow cherry tomatoes as well as the red.

Although I had seen tomatoes growing in garden greenhouses and in the fields of Italy and Greece, I had never seen tomato growing in Britain on a large scale until I started to write this book. When I walked into the magnificent glasshouses, I came across the lovely smell of the tomato plants and the gentle hum of the bees as they went about their work pollinating the tomato flowers. I have also discovered a few tips about handling tomatoes, their preparation and their cooking. I have passed these on to you in a hints and tips section and I hope these will be useful and will help you to enjoy the recipes. One of the main points to remember is that tomatoes are a subtropical fruit. They hate the cold, especially the refrigerator. To enjoy them at their best, serve them at room temperature. I keep tomatoes in the fruit bowl!

Victoria Lloyd-David

INTRODUCTION

The tomato is a berry and therefore a fruit but we use it as a vegetable. Tomatoes originate from South America. They were first cultivated by the Aztecs in the 16th century. Stories abound on how the tomato travelled from South America to southern Europe. Some say a Spanish priest brought seeds to Seville from Peru. Another legend tells us two Jesuit priests brought them to Italy from Mexico and that the first tomatoes were yellow, earning them the name *pomi d'oro* – golden apples of Italy. Southern Italy is still a big growing area and Italian cooking is based on *pomodora* – tomato dishes. The origin of the English word tomato comes from the Spanish word *tomate*. The French, convinced that the red berries had aphrodisiac qualities, called them *pomme d'amour* – love apples. Today, they are the most widely available vegetable in the world.

For many years tomatoes were grown in Britain and Europe as ornamental climbers. They were grown for their decorative leaves rather than their fruit. The first tomato grower on record in the UK was Patrick Bellow of Castletown who successfully reared plants from seeds in 1554. The Elizabethans thought the bright red colour of the fruit was a danger signal and that tomatoes were therefore harmful. Tomatoes are grown all over the world, from as far north as Iceland to the Southern tip of New Zealand.

CULTIVATED TOMATOES

It was not until the 19th century that commercial cultivation began. The first glasshouses were built in Kent and Essex in the mid-19th century when large scale production of sheet glass became possible. Today, these glasshouses cover vast areas of agricultural land. The largest single glasshouse, which covers 22 acres, is in the *Guinness Book of Records*.

Tomatoes (*Lycopersicon esculentum*) are now one of the main horticultural crops in Britain and northern Europe. Because the weather is unpredictable, and tomatoes are easily damaged by wind, extremes of temperature or fluctuating conditions, the growers have developed a system which maintains a constant environment for the plants.

The glasshouse offers a much longer growing season; it raises the temperature of the soil and air within; it provides shelter from the weather; and it protects the crop from birds and animals. The temperature, humidity, air, water, light and nutrients are all controlled to give ideal conditions. The plants are cultivated in the same way as in a garden greenhouse, except on a much

ABOVE: Tomatoes growing in Britain.

ABOVE: The bumble bee is the natural pollinator most widely used by British tomato growers.

larger scale. Walk into tomato glasshouses in Britain and you will hear the gentle buzz of bumble bees pollinating the tomato flowers. Rows of tomato plants stretch into the distance. Each plant will be green and healthy with trusses of tomatoes hanging from its stem. The fruit requires 40-60 days from flowering to reach full ripeness. The first tomatoes ripen low down the plant but as the season progresses , they ripen further up. All tomatoes are picked by hand. Predators are encouraged, rather than chemical sprays. Nature has created a bug-eat-bug world, so British tomato growers have harnessed beneficial insects to control pests.

CHOOSING TOMATOES

In Britain we eat approximately 5 kg (11 lbs) of tomatoes per person per year. The traditional round tomato is the most popular. It accounts for over 80% of tomato sales. They are good for grilling, baking or frying as a vegetable, used as a cooking ingredient for soups and sauces or eaten raw in salads.

Cherry and cocktail tomatoes are much smaller than the traditional round tomatoes. Cherry tomatoes are the smallest and cocktail tomatoes are slightly larger. Both are enjoyed for their sweetness and more concentrated flavour. Cherry tomatoes are best eaten whole and raw in salads; cocktail tomatoes can be halved for salads or skewered whole for grilling. Most cherry tomatoes are red but yellow ones are also available.

Beefsteak or beef tomatoes are much larger than the traditional round tomato. Their size and shape makes them excellent for stuffing and baking whole. Plum tomatoes have a distinctive oval shape with firm flesh and less liquid in the centre. These are ideal for Mediterranean dishes such as pizza, pasta and salads. More recent varieties of flavoursome tomatoes include Gourmet, Melrow, Flavia and Momatara.

Sun-dried tomatoes are dried naturally in the Mediterranean or Californian sun, then they are packed in glass jars with olive oil and sold as *pomodori secchi* or sun-dried tomatoes in oil. Others are packed dry in sealed cellophane bags. They can be added to hot or cold dishes, or simply spread over slices of ciabatta bread for a snack.

Canned, peeled tomatoes are probably one of the most popular convenience cooking ingredients. They are mainly Italian plum tomatoes, always peeled, often chopped, and sometimes mixed with herbs, flavourings or other vegetables such as peppers, onions and garlic. One Italian tomato cannery has recently celebrated its

ABOVE: (left to right) Cherry tomato, cocktail tomato, salad tomato, traditional round tomato, plum tomato, beefsteak tomato, Momatara beefsteak tomato.

ABOVE: *(clockwise from top left)* Passata, tomato juice, canned tomatoes, sundried tomatoes in oil, tomato flakes, sun-dried tomatoes, tomato purée.

centenary. There are plenty of other tomato products in shops and supermarkets.

Smooth, thick purées of tomatoes such as passata, come in jars; creamed tomatoes in cartons. They are natural in colour and flavour and have no additives. Once opened, they should be stored in the refrigerator. Salsina is a chunky mix of fresh, crushed tomatoes, packed in thick tomato juices.

Tomato paste is a double concentrate form of tomatoes sold in small cans or tubes. Some specialists make a paste with sun-dried tomatoes for an even more distinctive flavour. Tomato juice is sold in cartons as a refreshing long drink, or in small cans or bottles for mixer drinks, aperitifs and cocktails.

Tomato flakes and other new tomato products have recently come in to the shops. These are available from some supermarkets and from delicatessens.

Fresh tomato sauces can be found in supermarket chill cabinets.

BUYING TOMATOES

Tomatoes are available all year round. Choose firm tomatoes with bright, unflawed skins. They should be a good shape, good colour and have a smooth skin. When cut, they should be firm to the centre. There are two tests for freshness: one is the smell, which should be faintly aromatic; and the other is that the small grey-green leaves at the stalk end (known as the calyx) should not be too withered or dried.

Just-ripe tomatoes are best stored at room temperature as they are a subtropical fruit and they prefer warmth. Never keep tomatoes in the refrigerator, even over-ripe ones, as they will go soft more quickly in cold temperatures. Buy tomatoes regularly. If you have put them in a plastic bag, or if they are pre-packed, remove this packaging and place them in a bowl. Handle them with care.

To ripen home-grown tomatoes, place a ripe tomato in amongst the unripe ones. Keep them in a paper bag at room temperature and the ripe tomato will help ripen the others. Conversely, if you have a glut of over-ripe tomatoes, use them to make soups and sauces which can be stored in the freezer.

The end of season yellow or green slightly under-ripe traditional round tomatoes are most suitable for making chutneys.

NUTRITION

Low in calories. Tomatoes contain 14 calories per 100g.

Good source of vitamins. Tomatoes contain Vitamins A and C and when eaten raw, they also contain Vitamin E. Grilled tomatoes are high in carotene and folate.

Mineral content. Potassium and calcium together with mineral salts and trace elements. Grilled tomatoes contain a higher concentration of nutrients.

Dietary fibre. Tomatoes contribute dietary fibre when eaten raw with the skin and seeds.

PREPARATION

For salads, remove the stalk and rinse the tomatoes under cold running water. Dry them with kitchen paper. Before cooking whole tomatoes, make a cross in the skin over the top of the tomato with a sharp pointed knife. This will prevent the skin from splitting.

To peel tomatoes, make a 'nick' in the skin with a sharp knife. Then put in a bowl, cover with boiling water for one minute, drain, then pour over cold water. Take out the tomatoes, one at a time, and remove the skins with a sharp, pointed knife. There is no need to remove the core unless the tomato is very big.

If a recipe requires the use of a tomato as a shell, take a slice off the top of the tomato or slice in half, then gently scoop out the seeds with a teaspoon. Season the inside of the tomato. Turn upside down onto a piece of kitchen paper to allow the juices to drain off. Dry inside the tomato shells with kitchen paper.

Some recipes require that tomato seeds are removed when making tomato purée for it to be really smooth. Use a fine nylon or stainless steel sieve and press the tomato pulp through the mesh with a wooden spoon.

Home-made tomato juice is quick and easy. Chop the tomatoes, then liquidise in a blender or food processor. Strain the juice through a sieve.

Peeled and seeded tomatoes make excellent pulp or purée for cooking. Cook them slowly until reduced to the required consistency. Leave them to cool, then pour into freezer bags or ice-cube trays to freeze. Once frozen, transfer the cubes to freezer bags. These can be stored in the freezer for up to six months and used for soups, sauces and casseroles.

Tomatoes also make attractive garnishes. Always use a sharp vegetable knife. To make a **tomato flower**, make a series of 'v' shaped cuts or zig-zags around the middle of each tomato, pushing the knife tip right through to the centre. Carefully pull the two halves apart.

For a **tomato rose**, cut a slice from the base of the tomato and continue peeling the skin off in a spiral, taking care not to break the skin. Place a strip on a chopping board and loosely wind it to form a neat roll like the base of a rose and secure with a cocktail stick. Wind a second piece of skin tightly to form the centre of the rose. Place in the middle and secure with a cocktail stick.

For a **tomato tulip**, make six diagonal cuts into the skin from the core to half way down the tomato. Peel back the skin with a sharp knife.

ABOVE: (top) Tomato tulip; (left) tomato flower; (right) tomato rose.

The only preparation needed before using sun-dried tomatoes in oil is to drain them before use. The remaining oil can be used in the recipe or saved for a salad dressing mixed with a little balsamic vinegar, or in a stir fry. However, dried sun-dried tomatoes require soaking before use. Follow the packet instructions, but if you buy them loose from a delicatessen the general rule is to rinse them well, then soak them in warm water for 20 minutes. Strain, then use them on their own or with fresh tomatoes. Once opened, it is best to transfer the remaining dried tomatoes to a screw–topped jar and store them in the refrigerator. If the tomatoes are very tough or salty, refresh them in a few changes of hot water.

HINTS AND TIPS

☺ Always keep tomatoes at room temperature and not in the refrigerator. They are a subtropical fruit and they dislike the cold. Prepare salad tomatoes at least four hours before the meal.

☺ The natural herb partners for tomatoes are mint, parsley, basil and oregano. For the best flavour, use fresh herbs whenever possible.

☺ Season tomatoes with a pinch of sugar to bring out their natural sweetness.

☺ If a recipe requires the removal of seeds and juices, reserve these and use for stocks and sauces.

☺ Always drain tomato shells on kitchen paper and dry them out well before filling them.

☺ Tomatoes give food a good colour. Add some passata or tomato purée to paler dishes like chicken or fish.

☺ Always use a sharp knife to cut tomatoes. One with a fine serrated edge can be used as an alternative.

☺ If tomatoes are cooked with their skins they will retain more flavour.

☺ Put whole or halved tomatoes on skewers for a barbecue. Team them with other vegetables which cook quickly such as mushrooms, peppers or courgettes.

☺ Tomato seeds give a good texture to soups and sauces but if the recipe requires a smooth purée, it is important to sieve it. As tomatoes are an acid fruit, use a nylon or stainless steel sieve.

☺ Make a cross in the skin of the tomato before baking. Press a little crushed garlic or chopped herbs into the tomato, drizzle over some olive oil and cook at 190°C (375°F/Gas Mark 5) for 15-20 minutes.

☺ Brush tomatoes with oil or sprinkle over some breadcrumbs before grilling. Grill tomatoes slowly, otherwise the cut surface of the tomato will begin to burn before the tomato is heated through.

☺ Tomatoes get particularly hot in the microwave and in toasted sandwiches. Cool slightly before eating.

☺ Use sun-dried tomatoes in conjunction with fresh tomatoes to strengthen the tomato flavour of the dish.

☺ Put some halved tomatoes around roasted meat for the last 20 minutes of cooking time.

☺ Serve tomato juice with lots of ice. Add a dash of lemon juice, Worcestershire sauce or Tabasco if you like.

☺ Tomato juice is an excellent pick-me-up after a heavy night's eating and drinking.

☺ To turn tomato soup into a meal, cover it with a thick layer of grated mozzarella cheese and lots of chopped fresh basil. Serve with large slices of crusty bread.

☺ Home–made tomato soups and sauces can be stored in the freezer for up to six months.

☺ Use under-ripe or green tomatoes for making chutneys and pickles.

☺ Tomato pulp is said to be very good for the skin. It refreshes, tones and aids circulation and will restore acidity to the face after cleansing. Put peeled tomatoes and lemon juice in a blender or food processor and splash on the face. Rinse off with tepid water.

RIGHT: Tomato soup covered with a thick layer of mozzarella cheese and chopped fresh basil, served with crusty bread.

SOUPS AND STARTERS

'Real' tomato soup made with fresh tomatoes is easy to make and tastes delicious.
Because tomatoes work equally well hot or cold, they make tasty soups, mousses,
dips and pâtés, or can be stuffed with meat or vegetable fillings.

CLASSIC TOMATO SOUP

30 ml (2 tbsp) OLIVE OIL
1 kg (2 lbs) TOMATOES, HALVED
2 cloves GARLIC
1 SMALL POTATO, PEELED AND SLICED
5 ml (1 tsp) SUGAR

To garnish
20 ml (4 tsp) SINGLE CREAM
sprig PARSLEY

Pre-heat the oven to 190°C (375°F/Gas mark 5).
Lightly oil a roasting tin. Arrange the tomatoes, cut side
up in the roasting tin. Add the garlic cloves. Season and
drizzle over the remaining oil. Roast for 30 minutes.

Meanwhile, boil the potato in 300 ml (1/2 pint) water
until tender. Reserve the potato water. Skin the
tomatoes and garlic. Put the tomato pulp and garlic into
a blender or food processor with the cooked potato and
potato stock. Blend until smooth. Transfer to a
saucepan. Add a little extra stock or water if the soup is
too thick. Stir in the sugar and garnish.   SERVES 4

TOMATO AND ORANGE SOUP WITH BASIL

450 g (1 lb) TOMATOES, PEELED
1 ONION, SLICED
1 CARROT, SLICED
1 strip LEMON RIND
1 BAY LEAF
10 ml (2 tsp) CHOPPED FRESH BASIL OR
2.5 ml (1/2 tsp) DRIED BASIL
600 ml (1 pint) VEGETABLE STOCK
25 g (1 oz) BUTTER
25 g (1 oz) FLOUR
1 SMALL ORANGE

Halve the tomatoes and squeeze them to remove the
seeds. Put the tomatoes, onion and carrot in a saucepan
with the lemon rind, bay leaf and basil. Season. Add the
stock and simmer, covered, for about 1/2 hour.
Liquidise, cool and set aside.

Clean the pan, melt the butter, add the flour and cook
for a few minutes. Remove from the heat, then gradually
add the liquidised mixture. Bring to the boil. Peel the
orange. Finely shred the rind, blanch, then refresh in
cold water. Squeeze the orange and add the juice to the
soup. Check the seasoning and serve garnished with
orange rind.   SERVES 4

RIGHT: Classic Tomato Soup

ICED TOMATO SOUP

450 g (1 lb) TOMATOES, PEELED AND THINLY SLICED
4 SPRING ONIONS, THINLY SLICED
4 cloves GARLIC, FINELY CHOPPED
strip LEMON RIND
45 ml (3 tbsp) TOMATO PURÉE
30 ml (2 tbsp) FLOUR
600 ml (1 pint) CHICKEN STOCK
5 ml (1 tsp) HOT PEPPER SAUCE
5 ml (1 tsp) SUGAR
30 ml (2 tbsp) SHERRY (OPTIONAL)
5 ml (1 tsp) LEMON JUICE
150 ml (5 fl oz) SINGLE CREAM
thin slices CUCUMBER, TO GARNISH

Put the tomatoes, onions, garlic, lemon rind and 60 ml (4 tbsp) water in a saucepan. Simmer gently for 10-15 minutes. Add the tomato purée and cook for a further 3 minutes. Make a paste with the flour and some of the stock, then stir it in. Add the remaining stock, hot pepper sauce and sugar. Season. Bring to the boil, stirring. Sieve the soup through a fine strainer. Add sherry (if desired), and lemon juice. Add the cream and refrigerate until very cold. Serve garnished with thin cucumber slices. SERVES 6-8

GAZPACHO

1 CUCUMBER
450 g (1 lb) TOMATOES, PEELED
1 LARGE GREEN PEPPER, SEEDED
1 ONION
1 clove GARLIC, CRUSHED
45-60 ml (3-4 tbsp) OIL
45-60 ml (3-4 tbsp) WINE VINEGAR
1 x 415 ml (14.6 fl oz) CAN TOMATO JUICE
30 ml (2 tbsp) TOMATO PURÉE

Roughly chop the cucumber, tomatoes, pepper and onion. Reserve some vegetables for the garnish and chop these more finely. Put the roughly chopped vegetables and garlic into a bowl. Add the remaining ingredients. Purée in small amounts in a blender or food processor. Pour into a bowl. Cover and chill well. Serve in soup bowls garnished with the reserved vegetables.

SERVES 6

TOP: *Iced Tomato Soup*
BOTTOM: *Gazpacho*

QUICK STUFFED TOMATOES

✿

6 LARGE TOMATOES
2 RIPE AVOCADOS
115 g (4 oz) CREAM CHEESE
5 ml (1 tsp) HORSERADISH SAUCE
5 ml (1 tsp) LEMON JUICE
5 ml (1 tsp) GARLIC PURÉE
6 slices RYE BREAD

Use a sharp knife to cut a very thin slice to remove the top of each tomato. Scoop out the flesh with a small teaspoon. Halve the avocados, discard the stones and scoop out the flesh. Place the avocado in a small bowl with the cream cheese and horseradish sauce. Beat until smooth. Add lemon juice and garlic purée. Season. Place in a piping bag with a small rosette piping nozzle. Fill the tomatoes with the avocado mixture and place each one on a base of rye bread. Pipe the remaining avocado mixture around the base of each tomato. Serve at room temperature. SERVES 6

HOT STUFFED TOMATOES

✿

4 BEEF TOMATOES
15 ml (1 tbsp) OLIVE OIL
1 MEDIUM ONION, PEELED AND FINELY CHOPPED
1 small clove GARLIC, CRUSHED
2 sticks CELERY, FINELY CHOPPED
45 g (1½ oz) FRESH WHOLEMEAL BREADCRUMBS
15 ml (1 tbsp) CHOPPED FRESH HERBS (BASIL, OREGANO, MARJORAM)

Preheat the oven to 180°C (350°F/Gas mark 4). Stand the tomatoes on their stem ends and slice off the top quarter. Remove the pulp with a small spoon and reserve. Stand the tomatoes upside down to drain.

Heat the oil in a pan and fry the onion, garlic and celery until soft but not browned. Stir in the breadcrumbs, herbs and tomato pulp. Season well. Fill the tomato cases with the mixture and replace the tops. Bake for about 20 minutes. Serve hot. SERVES 4

RIGHT: Hot Stuffed Tomatoes

CHERRY TOMATOES WITH RED PEPPER AND ORANGE

1 RED PEPPER, SEEDED AND QUARTERED

20 g (¾ oz) PACKET ASPIC POWDER

1 LARGE ORANGE, GRATED RIND RESERVED,
PEELED AND CHOPPED

250 g (9 oz) CHERRY TOMATOES, RESERVE 3,
PEEL AND SLICE REMAINDER

few sprigs FRESH CHERVIL

225 ml (8 fl oz) TOMATO JUICE

10 ml (2 tsp) CORIANDER SEEDS, TOASTED
AND CRUSHED

ORANGE SLICES AND FRESH CHERVIL

Grill the pepper until the skin is charred, then place in a plastic bag. Set aside for 20 minutes. Peel and cut the pepper into thin strips. Dissolve the aspic in 225 ml (8 fl oz) boiling water. Stir the grated orange rind into the aspic. Place a spoonful of aspic in the base of 6 individual moulds or ramekins. Chill until set.

Slice the reserved tomatoes into wedges and arrange on the aspic with the chervil. Carefully spoon over a little more aspic. Chill until set. Make the aspic up to 400 ml (14 fl oz) with the tomato juice and stir in the coriander seeds. Arrange the orange pieces on top of the aspic, spoon over a little tomato aspic. Chill until set. Layer the tomatoes on top of the oranges with the red pepper and tomato aspic. Chill until set.

To serve, dip the moulds in hot water for a few seconds, invert onto plates and garnish. SERVES 6

TOMATO AND LIME MOUSSE

2 (size 2) EGGS, SEPARATED

200 ml (7 fl oz) PASSATA

45 ml (3 tbsp) TOMATO PURÉE

grated rind and juice 1 LARGE LIME

15 ml (1 tbsp) POWDERED GELATINE

250 g (9 oz) MASCARPONE CHEESE

30 ml (2 tbsp) CHOPPED FRESH CORIANDER

Sauce

450 g (1 lb) TOMATOES, PEELED, SEEDED
AND CHOPPED

1 clove GARLIC, CRUSHED

30 ml (2 tbsp) OLIVE OIL

sprig PARSLEY

LIME SLICES AND FRESH CORIANDER,
TO GARNISH

Beat the egg yolks into the passata. Cook over a gentle heat until the mixture thickens. Do not allow to boil. Beat in the tomato purée and lime rind. Sprinkle the gelatine onto the lime juice. Leave to soak for 5 minutes, then dissolve over a pan of hot water. Cool. Whisk the gelatine mixture into the tomato mixture with the cheese and coriander. Season. When just beginning to set, whisk the egg whites until stiff, then fold into the tomato mixture. Turn into a wetted 900 g (2 lb) loaf tin and chill until set.

Meanwhile, put all the ingredients for the sauce in a saucepan. Season. Cover and simmer for 30 minutes. Remove the parsley, then strain the mixture through a nylon sieve into a jug. Chill.

Dip the mould into hot water for a few seconds then invert onto a board. Slice the mousse, garnish and serve with the chilled tomato sauce. SERVES 6

TOP: *Cherry Tomatoes with Red Pepper and Orange*

BOTTOM: *Tomato and Lime Mousse*

GUACAMOLE

❉

2 RIPE AVOCADOS, STONED AND PEELED

30 ml (2 tbsp) LEMON JUICE

25 g (1 oz) SPRING ONION, VERY FINELY CHOPPED

2 cloves GARLIC, CRUSHED

1.25-2.5 ml (¼-½ tsp) HOT PEPPER SAUCE

pinch CHILLI POWDER

2 TOMATOES, PEELED, SEEDED AND VERY FINELY CHOPPED

TORTILLA CHIPS, TO SERVE

Mash the avocados into a purée with the lemon juice. Stir in the remaining ingredients. Turn into a serving dish, cover with cling film and refrigerate for 1 hour. Serve with tortilla chips.

SERVES 4-6

SUN-DRIED TOMATO AND GOAT'S CHEESE PÂTÉ

❉

85 g (3 oz) SUN-DRIED TOMATOES, SOAKED

225 g (8 oz) SOFT GOAT'S CHEESE

55 g (2 oz) PECAN NUTS OR WALNUTS, ROUGHLY CHOPPED

To serve

FRESHLY CHOPPED BASIL

CIABATTA BREAD, TOASTED OR WHOLEGRAIN BREAD

Place the goat's cheese and two thirds of the tomatoes in a blender or food processor and blend until almost smooth. Add the remaining tomatoes and blend to break them up, but allow them to remain textured. Transfer to a bowl and add the nuts. Stir to mix well. Turn the pâté into individual pâté dishes or into a serving dish. Chill.

To serve, sprinkle fresh basil on top of the pâté and accompany with toasted ciabatta or wholegrain bread.

SERVES 4

Top: Guacamole

Bottom: Sun-dried Tomato and Goat's Cheese Pâté

SALADS

Always serve tomatoes at room temperature. Bring out their natural sweetness with a pinch of sugar and choose a dressing which will not smother their flavour. Drizzle over a good quality olive oil and add freshly chopped herbs.

CLASSIC TOMATO SALAD

To ensure the tomatoes are at room temperature, remove from the refrigerator 8 hours before preparing the salad.

450 g (1 lb) TOMATOES
2.5 ml (¹/₂ tsp) CASTER SUGAR
1.25 ml (¹/₄ tsp) SALT
1.25 ml (¹/₄ tsp) GROUND BLACK PEPPER
30 ml (2 tbsp) EXTRA VIRGIN OLIVE OIL
10 ml (2 tsp) WHITE WINE VINEGAR
15 ml (1 tbsp) CHOPPED CHIVES

Thinly slice the tomatoes, discarding ends, and arrange on a plate. Sprinkle over the sugar, salt and pepper. Set aside for 30 minutes at room temperature. Whisk the oil and vinegar together and drizzle over the tomatoes. Sprinkle over the chives. Leave for another 30 minutes before serving.

SERVES 4

TOMATO AND MOZZARELLA SALAD

25 g (1 oz) PINE NUTS (OPTIONAL)
700 g (1¹/₂ lb) TOMATOES
350 g (12 oz) MOZZARELLA CHEESE
30 ml (2 tbsp) BASIL LEAVES
60 ml (4 tbsp) EXTRA VIRGIN OLIVE OIL

Toast the pine nuts (if using) until pale golden. Slice the tomatoes and mozzarella cheese. Arrange on serving plates and season. Chop the larger basil leaves, or keep small leaves whole, then scatter them over the tomatoes and cheese. Drizzle over the olive oil. Sprinkle on the toasted pine nuts if desired. Serve with warm ciabatta or French bread.

SERVES 4

TOP: Classic Tomato Salad
BOTTOM: Tomato and Mozzarella Salad

MEDITERRANEAN TRICOLORE SALAD

2 GREEN PEPPERS
2 RED PEPPERS
2 YELLOW PEPPERS

Dressing
90 ml (6 tbsp) OLIVE OIL
30 ml (2 tbsp) RED WINE VINEGAR
2 cloves GARLIC, CRUSHED

To serve
450 g (1 lb) BEEF TOMATOES
4 BASIL LEAVES, SHREDDED

Grill the peppers until the skin is blistered and charred, turning them so they blister all round. Place them in a plastic bag and set aside for 20 minutes. Peel off the skins, cut away the core and discard the seeds. Slice the peppers and put them in a dish. Whisk all the dressing ingredients together. Season. Pour over the peppers and leave to marinate for 1 hour.

Slice the tomatoes and arrange on a serving dish. Pile the peppers in the centre and scatter over the shredded basil leaves. SERVES 4

MEXICAN SALAD WITH CHILLI DRESSING

2 LARGE ORANGES
4 SMALL HEADS CHICORY
4 LARGE TOMATOES
1 SMALL GREEN CHILLI, SEEDED

Dressing
45 ml (3 tbsp) NATURAL YOGURT
45 ml (3 tbsp) MAYONNAISE
5-10 ml (1-2 tsp) CHILLI SAUCE
pinch CHILLI POWDER
sprigs FRESH DILL, TO GARNISH

Peel the oranges and remove the white pith. Cut the oranges into thin slices, discarding any pips. Cut the heads of chicory in half lengthways. Cut the tomatoes into wedges. Arrange the orange slices, chicory spears and tomatoes on 4 individual plates. Chop the chilli and sprinkle over the top. Mix all the dressing ingredients together and spoon a little over each salad. Serve any remaining dressing separately. Garnish with dill.

SERVES 4

RIGHT: Mediterranean Tricolore Salad

TOMATO AND CHICORY SALAD

450 g (1 lb) COCKTAIL TOMATOES, QUARTERED
1 head CHICORY

Dressing
45 ml (3 tbsp) WALNUT OIL
15 ml (1 tbsp) BALSAMIC VINEGAR
juice of ½ LEMON
2.5 ml (½ tsp) CASTER SUGAR

Put the tomatoes in a bowl. Slice the chicory spear, discarding the end. Add the sliced chicory to the tomatoes. Whisk the dressing ingredients together and pour over the tomatoes. Season. Leave to marinate for 1 hour.

SERVES 4

WARM TOMATO SALAD

30 ml (2 tbsp) OLIVE OIL
450 g (1 lb) CHERRY TOMATOES
5 ml (1 tsp) CASTER SUGAR
100 g (3½ oz) MIXED GREEN SALAD
15 ml (1 tbsp) BALSAMIC VINEGAR

Heat the oil in a frying pan. Add the tomatoes and sugar and stir and shake over a moderate heat for 2-3 minutes until the tomato skins begin to split. Spoon the tomatoes over the green salad. Sprinkle over the vinegar. Toss and serve immediately.

SERVES 4

TOMATO AND AVOCADO SALAD

350 g (12 oz) TOMATOES, SLICED
1 bunch SPRING ONIONS, TRIMMED AND DIAGONALLY SLICED
2 AVOCADOS
juice 1 LEMON

Dressing
45 ml (3 tbsp) OLIVE OIL
30 ml (2 tbsp) RED WINE VINEGAR
10 ml (2 tsp) HONEY
10 ml (2 tsp) DIJON MUSTARD

Put the tomatoes and spring onions in a bowl and season. Peel the avocados, halve, discard the stone and slice. Squeeze over the lemon juice to prevent them browning. Gently mix the avocados with the tomatoes and onions. Put the olive oil, red wine vinegar, honey and mustard in a screw-topped jar, then shake vigorously to mix. Gently toss into the salad and serve.

SERVES 4

TOP: *Tomato and Chicory Salad*
BOTTOM: *Warm Tomato Salad*

PASTA SALAD

❦

175 g (6 oz) PASTA SHAPES
175 g (6 oz) COCKTAIL TOMATOES, HALVED
225 g (8 oz) TOMATOES, PEELED
2 SMALL COURGETTES, THINLY SLICED

Dressing
60 ml (4 tbsp) OLIVE OIL
15 ml (1 tbsp) RED WINE VINEGAR
1 clove GARLIC, CRUSHED
15 ml (1 tbsp) SHREDDED BASIL LEAVES

Cook the pasta in boiling salted water for about 5 minutes, until *al dente*. Drain and rinse in cold water, then drain again. Put the pasta in a bowl with the cocktail tomatoes. Quarter the other tomatoes, remove seeds then cut each quarter in half. Add to the salad with the courgettes. Mix the dressing, season, then pour over the salad. Cover and chill for 1 hour in the refrigerator. Just before serving, stir in the shredded basil. SERVES 6

COCKTAIL TOMATO AND BLUE CHEESE SALAD

❦

225 g (8 oz) RINDLESS SMOKED STREAKY BACON
1 ROUND LETTUCE
450 g (1 lb) COCKTAIL TOMATOES
1 bunch WATERCRESS
2 AVOCADOS
juice 1 LEMON
225 g (8 oz) GORGONZOLA CHEESE, FINELY SLICED
60 ml (4 tbsp) OLIVE OIL
30 ml (2 tbsp) RED WINE VINEGAR
10 ml (2 tsp) HONEY
5 ml (1 tsp) AMERICAN MUSTARD

Grill the bacon until crisp, drain on kitchen paper then finely chop. Separate, wash and dry the lettuce, halve the tomatoes, trim and wash the watercress. Mix the bacon, lettuce, tomatoes and watercress together. Peel and slice the avocados, then squeeze the lemon juice over to stop them browning. Toss into the salad. Gently stir the cheese into the salad. Mix the olive oil and red wine vinegar. Add the honey and mustard and season. Toss into the salad. Arrange on serving plates and scatter over the crispy bacon pieces. SERVES 4

RIGHT: Cocktail Tomato and Blue Cheese Salad

SANDWICHES AND SNACKS

The tomato is a truly portable food and is ideal for taking on picnics. Sandwiches can be made using tomato breads, where the tomatoes are baked with the dough. The chapter also includes bagels, muffins and toasted sandwiches – plenty of ideas for snacks, brunches and lunch boxes.

BLT

1 RASHER SMOKED STREAKY BACON
15 g (¹/₂ oz) LOW FAT SPREAD
2 slices WHOLEGRAIN MALTED BREAD
10 ml (2 tsp) MAYONNAISE
1 TOMATO, SLICED
2 WEBB'S LETTUCE LEAVES

Grill the bacon until it is really crisp. Cool on kitchen paper, then cut rasher in half. Spread low fat spread on 1 side of each slice of bread. Repeat for the mayonnaise. Arrange the bacon on 1 slice of bread, top with the sliced tomato and lettuce leaves. Put the other slice of bread on top. Press down gently and cut sandwich into 2 triangles.

MAKES 1 SANDWICH

SMOKED SALMON AND TOMATO BAGEL

1 BAGEL
15 ml (1 tbsp) MASCARPONE CHEESE
25 g (1 oz) SMOKED SALMON
1 TOMATO, THINLY SLICED
GROUND BLACK PEPPER
2 sprigs FRESH DILL

Slice the bagel in half horizontally. Spread both sides with mascarpone cheese. Top 1 side with smoked salmon, tomato, black pepper and dill. Place the other half of the bagel on top.

SERVES 1

Top: BLT

BOTTOM: Smoked Salmon and Tomato Bagel

TOASTED GRUYÈRE AND TOMATO SANDWICH

2 THICK SLICES WHITE BREAD
15 g (½ oz) SLICE GRUYÈRE OR GOUDA CHEESE
25 g (1 oz) AMERICAN STYLE WAFER-THIN HAM
1 TOMATO, SLICED
5 ml (1 tsp) GROUNDNUT OIL

Heat the sandwich toaster. Meanwhile, place a slice of bread down on a board, top with the cheese, then ham, followed by sliced tomato. Place the second slice of bread on top and press down firmly. Lightly oil the heated sandwich toaster. Place sandwich in toaster. Cover and cook for approximately 3 minutes or until the bread is golden and crisp.   MAKES 1 SANDWICH

TOMATO AND MUSHROOM MUFFINS

115 g (4 oz) CLOSED CUP MUSHROOMS, SLICED
5 ml (1 tsp) WORCESTERSHIRE SAUCE
5 ml (1 tsp) WHOLE GRAIN MUSTARD
1 WHOLEMEAL MUFFIN
2 TOMATOES, SLICED

Put the mushrooms, 30 ml (2 tbsp) water, the Worcestershire sauce and mustard together in a small saucepan. Simmer over a gentle heat, stirring occasionally.

Meanwhile, split the muffin in half and toast on both sides. Top each half with sliced tomato and grill until heated through. Spoon the mushroom mixture over the top.   SERVES 2

RIGHT: Tomato and Mushroom Muffins

AUBERGINE AND MOZZARELLA BITES

It is important that the aubergine and tomatoes are approximately the same circumference when sliced.

1 AUBERGINE
60 ml (4 tbsp) PASSATA
115 g (4 oz) MOZZARELLA CHEESE, GRATED
2 BEEF TOMATOES, PEELED AND SLICED
10-12 BASIL LEAVES
15 ml (1 tbsp) OLIVE OIL

Slice the aubergine into 1 cm (¹/₂ inch) slices. Sprinkle with salt and set aside for half hour. Drain and dry with kitchen paper.

Pre-heat the oven to 220°C (425°F/Gas mark 7). Arrange the aubergine slices on a greased baking tray. Spread 5 ml (1 tsp) of passata on each aubergine slice. Top with mozzarella, tomato slices and basil leaves. Season. Drizzle a little oil over each basil leaf. Bake for 15 minutes. Cool for 1 minute before serving.

MAKES 10-12

CROSTINI

700 g (1¹/₂ lb) PLUM TOMATOES, PEELED, SEEDED AND FINELY CHOPPED
3 cloves GARLIC, FINELY CHOPPED
8 BASIL LEAVES, CHOPPED
60 ml (4 tbsp) EXTRA VIRGIN OLIVE OIL
3 ANCHOVIES, DRAINED AND FINELY CHOPPED
115 g (4 oz) BLACK OLIVES, PITTED AND FINELY CHOPPED
1 loaf CIABATTA BREAD
115 g (4 oz) MOZZARELLA CHEESE, GRATED

Put the tomatoes, garlic and basil in a bowl. Add the olive oil and stir well. Marinate at room temperature for 1 hour.

Pre-heat the oven to 200°C (400°F/Gas mark 6). Stir in the anchovies and black olives. Cut the bread into thick slices. Arrange on a baking sheet. Bake for 10 minutes. Remove the bread from the oven and turn the grill to high. Sprinkle the cheese over the bread and grill for 1 minute. Spoon the tomato mixture over the cheese and grill for a further 2 minutes. Serve warm.

MAKES 16-18 SLICES

RIGHT: Aubergine and Mozzarella Bites, Crostini

TOMATO FOCACCIA

55 g (2 oz) DRIED SUN-DRIED TOMATOES,
SOAKED FOR 20 MINUTES

350 g (12 oz) STRONG PLAIN WHITE FLOUR

2.5 ml (1/2 tsp) SALT

10 ml (2 tsp) EASY BLEND DRIED YEAST

75 ml (3 fl oz) OLIVE OIL

Topping

45 ml (3 tbsp) OLIVE OIL

15 ml (1 tbsp) SEA SALT

15 ml (1 tbsp) CHOPPED FRESH BASIL

15 ml (1 tbsp) CHOPPED FRESH THYME

Drain the tomatoes well, then finely chop. Sieve the flour and salt together into a warm bowl, then stir in the dried yeast. Add the oil, 150 ml (1/4 pint) warm water and tomatoes. Mix well. Knead on a lightly floured surface for 5 minutes. Roll out a rectangle 28 x 15 cm (11 x 6 inches). Place on a lightly oiled baking sheet. Make about 20 deep thumb indentations in the dough. Brush with the olive oil, cover with cling film and leave in a warm place for about 40 minutes.

Pre-heat the oven to 220°C (425°F/Gas mark 7).

Mix the topping ingredients together. Sprinkle over the dough. Bake for about 20 minutes. Best eaten warm.

MAKES 1 LOAF

SUN-DRIED TOMATO LOAF

225 g (8 oz) STRONG PLAIN WHITE FLOUR

2.5 ml (1/2 tsp) SALT

7.5 ml (1 1/2 tsp) EASY BLEND DRIED YEAST

55 g (2 oz) SUN-DRIED TOMATOES IN OIL,
DRAINED AND VERY FINELY CHOPPED

30 ml (2 tbsp) OIL FROM THE TOMATO JAR

15 ml (1 tbsp) FINELY CHOPPED FRESH ROSEMARY

Sieve the flour and salt into a warm bowl. Stir in the yeast with the remaining ingredients and add 142 ml (1/4 pint) warm water. Mix well. Knead on a lightly floured surface for 5 minutes. Place in a lightly oiled 450 g (1 lb) loaf tin. Cover with cling film then leave in a warm place until double in size.

Pre-heat the oven to 220°C (425°F/Gas mark 7).

Dust the top of the risen loaf with flour, then bake for about 20 minutes until well risen and golden brown. The base should sound hollow when tapped.

MAKES 1 LOAF

TOP: Tomato Focaccia
BOTTOM: Sun-dried Tomato Loaf

TOMATO AND GARLIC MINI ROLLS

The mini rolls are pictured on page 71 alongside Spiced Roast Beef with Tomato and Ginger Sauce.

25 g (1 oz) DRIED TOMATO FLAKES,
    SOAKED FOR 30 MINUTES
225 g (8 oz) STRONG PLAIN BROWN FLOUR
2.5 ml (1/2 tsp) SALT
25 g (1 oz) BUTTER
7.5 ml (1 1/2 tsp) EASY BLEND DRIED YEAST
1-2 cloves GARLIC, CRUSHED

To Glaze
BEATEN EGG
SESAME SEEDS

Drain the tomato flakes well. Sieve the flour and salt together into a warm bowl. Rub in the butter and stir in the yeast. Add the garlic and tomato flakes, then add up to 125-150 ml (approx. 1/4 pint) warm water to form a soft, but not sticky, dough. Knead on a lightly floured surface for 5 minutes. Divide the dough into 12 and shape into 10 cm (4 inch) rolls. Make 3 deep scissor snips down the length of each roll. Place on a lightly oiled baking sheet. Cover with oiled cling film and leave in a warm place until double in size.

Pre-heat the oven to 220°C (425°F/Gas mark 7). Brush the rolls with beaten egg, then sprinkle sesame seeds over the top. Bake for about 12 minutes.

MAKES 12 ROLLS

MEXICAN TACOS

30 ml (2 tbsp) OIL
1 ONION, CHOPPED
2 cloves GARLIC, CHOPPED
450 g (1 lb) TOMATOES, PEELED AND CHOPPED
2 GREEN CHILLIES, SEEDED AND SLICED
2.5 ml (1/2 tsp) HOT PEPPER SAUCE
175 g (6 oz) COOKED CHICKEN, DICED
8 TACO SHELLS
85 g (3 oz) SHREDDED LETTUCE
55 g (2 oz) CHEDDAR CHEESE, GRATED
8 BLACK OLIVES

Heat the oil in a pan and cook the onion and garlic gently for 3 minutes. Add the tomatoes, chillies and hot pepper sauce. Cover and simmer very gently, for 12 minutes until the sauce is reduced to a pulp. Stir in the chicken. Remove from heat. Cover and set aside for 1 hour to allow the flavours to blend.

Pre-heat the oven to 180°C (350°F/Gas mark 4). Heat the taco shells for 2-3 minutes. Meanwhile, reheat the tomato mixture. Divide the shredded lettuce between each taco shell. Spoon over the tomato mixture. Sprinkle over the grated cheese and top each taco with an olive.

MAKES 8 TACOS

RIGHT: Mexican Tacos

CHEESE-STUFFED TOMATOES

12 TOMATOES
225 g (8 oz) GRUYÈRE CHEESE, GRATED
5 ml (1 tsp) FRENCH MUSTARD
1 clove GARLIC, CRUSHED
good pinch CAYENNE PEPPER
5 ml (1 tsp) WHITE WINE
45 g (1½ oz) FRESH WHITE BREADCRUMBS
15 ml (1 tbsp) OLIVE OIL
4 slices TOAST, TO SERVE

Pre-heat the oven to 180°C (350°F/Gas mark 4). Cut the tops off the tomatoes and scoop out the seeds and flesh. Season the tomato insides with salt and pepper, then stand upside down to drain. Heat the cheese very gently in a pan. Remove from heat and stir in the mustard, garlic, cayenne and white wine.

Arrange the tomatoes in a greased roasting tin. Fill each tomato with the cheese mixture, sprinkle over the breadcrumbs and drizzle over the oil. Bake for 15-20 minutes. Serve on toast with vegetables or salad.

SERVES 4

STUFFED BEEF TOMATOES

4 LARGE BEEF TOMATOES
2 RASHERS STREAKY BACON
115 g (4 oz) CHESTNUT MUSHROOMS, FINELY CHOPPED
4 (size 4) EGGS
25 g (1 oz) BUTTER
4 slices TOAST, TO SERVE

Pre-heat the oven to 180°C (350°F/Gas mark 4). Cut the tops off the tomatoes and scoop out the seeds and flesh. Season the tomato insides with salt and pepper, then stand upside down to drain. Dry fry the bacon until crisp. Remove from the pan and set aside. Put the mushrooms in the pan and cook quickly until crisp and golden. Remove from heat. Chop the bacon.

Place the tomatoes in a greased ovenproof dish. Divide the bacon and mushrooms between the tomatoes and gently break an egg into each tomato. Dot with butter and bake for 15-18 minutes, until the eggs are set. Serve with toast.

SERVES 4

TOP: Cheese-stuffed Tomatoes
BOTTOM: Stuffed Beef Tomatoes

FAMILY MEALS

Tomatoes complement pizza, pasta, omelettes and cheese dishes. The family will also enjoy Crispy Bacon Filo Pie, Devilled Chicken Baked in Foil and Hungarian Goulash, or a variation on macaroni cheese, spiced up with Worcestershire sauce and a pinch of cayenne pepper.

TOMATO PIZZA

Pizza Base
15 g (1/2 oz) FRESH YEAST
250 g (9 oz) PLAIN STRONG FLOUR
5 ml (1 tsp) SALT
30 ml (2 tbsp) OLIVE OIL
60 ml (4 tbsp) MILK

Topping
1 kg (2 lb) PLUM TOMATOES, PEELED
60 ml (4 tbsp) OLIVE OIL
2 cloves GARLIC, CRUSHED
115 g (4 oz) MOZZARELLA CHEESE, CHOPPED
10 ml (2 tsp) OREGANO, CHOPPED
1 x 55 g (2 oz) CAN ANCHOVY FILLETS (OPTIONAL)

Slice half the tomatoes and chop the remainder. Heat half the oil in a pan and fry the garlic for 30 seconds. Add the chopped tomatoes. Cover and simmer for 10 minutes, until reduced to a dry pulp. Season and cool.

Make the pizza base. Cream the fresh yeast with 30 ml (2 tbsp) warm water. Sift the flour and salt into a bowl, make a well in the centre and pour in the yeast mix, oil and half the milk. Mix to a firm dough adding more milk if necessary. Knead for 5 minutes.

Pre-heat the oven to 220°C (425°F/Gas mark 7). Cover and leave the dough to rise in a warm place until double in size.

Knead the dough for 2 minutes, cut it in half, roll each piece into a 20-23 cm (8-9 inch) circle. Place the pizza bases on oiled trays. Brush with oil. Cover with the tomato pulp. Arrange the fresh tomato slices over each pizza. Sprinkle over the mozzarella and oregano. Drizzle the remaining oil over the pizzas and bake for 20-25 minutes.

If adding the anchovies, drain them and use a sharp knife to slit each fillet in half lengthways. Arrange the anchovy fillets on the pizzas before the mozzarella.

RIGHT: Tomato Pizza

CRISPY BACON FILO PIE

85 g *(3 oz)* UNSALTED BUTTER

15 ml *(1 tbsp)* OIL

2 LARGE ONIONS, THINLY SLICED

15 ml *(1 tbsp)* CUMIN SEEDS

225 g *(8 oz)* PACKET FILO PASTRY

45 ml *(3 tbsp)* SEMOLINA

450 g *(1 lb)* PLUM TOMATOES, PEELED, QUARTERED AND SEEDED

450 g *(1 lb)* UNSMOKED BACK BACON RASHERS, GRILLED UNTIL FAIRLY CRISP

Melt 25 g (1 oz) of the butter with the oil. Add the onions and cook in a covered pan for 15-20 minutes, stirring occasionally, until golden brown. Stir in the cumin seeds and cook for 1 minute. Melt the remaining butter.

Pre-heat the oven to 190°C (375°F/Gas mark 5). Arrange 9 pastry sheets in a 25 cm (9 inch) loose-bottomed flan tin, so that about one third of each sheet is left hanging over the edge. Brush each with a little melted butter. Sprinkle semolina over the base, then top with the tomatoes, bacon and cooked onions. Bring the pastry up and arrange in loose folds over the filling. Arrange the remaining sheets on top in loose folds to completely cover the filling, brushing with butter while folding the pastry. Bake for 25-30 minutes. SERVES 4

TOMATO AND CHEESE PICNIC PIE

350 g *(12 oz)* SHORTCRUST PASTRY

30 ml *(2 tbsp)* OIL

1 SMALL ONION, THINLY SLICED

30 ml *(2 tbsp)* FLOUR

good pinch BLACK PEPPER AND MUSTARD POWDER

350 g *(12 oz)* TOMATOES, PEELED AND SLICED

175 g *(6 oz)* CHEDDAR CHEESE, GRATED

MILK FOR BRUSHING

Pre-heat the oven to 200°C (400°F/Gas mark 6). Divide the pastry in two. Use half to line a 23 cm (9 inch) pie plate. Reserve the other half for the lid.

Heat the oil and fry the onion until soft and lightly golden. Meanwhile, mix the flour, pepper and mustard powder together. Stir into the softened onions and add the tomatoes. Mix well. Arrange half the cheese over the pastry base, cover with the tomato mixture, then the rest of the cheese. Cover with the pastry lid, seal the edges well, brush the top with milk and bake for 30 minutes. Allow to cool. Serve cold. SERVES 4-6

TOP: Crispy Bacon Filo Pie

BOTTOM: Tomato and Cheese Picnic Pie

PIQUANT LAMB

♨

225 g (8 oz) TOMATOES, PEELED AND CHOPPED
1 LARGE ONION, SLICED INTO THIN WEDGES
45 ml (3 tbsp) STOCK
3 BAY LEAVES
350 g (12 oz) LEAN LAMB, CUT INTO STRIPS
350 g (12 oz) CLOSED CUP MUSHROOMS, HALVED
225 g (8 oz) CARROTS, CUT INTO THICK STICKS
30 ml (2 tbsp) CAPERS
30 ml (2 tbsp) TOMATO PURÉE

Place the tomatoes, onion, stock, bay leaves and lamb in a large frying pan. Bring to the boil, cover and simmer for 5 minutes. Add the mushrooms and cook for 10 minutes. Add the carrots and capers and cook for a further 5 minutes. Stir in the tomato purée.

Cook uncovered, over a high heat for 2-3 minutes to reduce some of the liquid. Remove the bay leaves before serving.

SERVES 4

GREEK STUFFED TOMATOES

♨

8 BEEF TOMATOES
30 ml (2 tbsp) OLIVE OIL
1 ONION, FINELY CHOPPED
1 clove GARLIC, CHOPPED
250 g (9 oz) RISOTTO RICE
1 litre (1³/4 pint) HOT CHICKEN STOCK
225 g (8 oz) COOKED LAMB, FINELY CHOPPED
30 ml (2 tbsp) CURRANTS
15 ml (1 tbsp) FRESH THYME

Pre-heat the oven to 180°C (350°F/Gas mark 4).

Cut the tops off the tomatoes and scoop out the seeds and flesh. Season the tomato insides with salt and pepper, then stand them upside down to drain.

Heat half the oil in a pan and cook the onion and garlic for 2 minutes. Add the rice and stir over a low heat for 2 minutes. Add 300 ml (1/2 pint) of the stock and cook gently, stirring, until the liquid has been absorbed. Repeat as before with the next 300 ml (1/2 pint) of stock and again with the final amount of stock. Stir in the lamb, currants and thyme.

Arrange the tomatoes in a greased roasting tin. Fill each tomato with the rice mixture. Drizzle over the remaining oil. Bake for 30 minutes.

SERVES 4

TOP: *Piquant Lamb*
BOTTOM: *Greek Stuffed Tomatoes*

DEVILLED CHICKEN BAKED IN FOIL

4 SUN-DRIED TOMATOES IN OIL, DRAINED
AND CHOPPED
60 ml (4 tbsp) TOMATO CHUTNEY
15 ml (1 tbsp) WHOLE GRAIN MUSTARD
55 g (2 oz) FRESH WHITE BREADCRUMBS
4 BONELESS CHICKEN BREASTS, SKINNED
20 ml (4 tsp) OIL FROM JAR OF SUN-DRIED TOMATOES
4 PIECES FOIL

Pre-heat the oven to 190°C (275°F/Gas mark 5). Mix the sun-dried tomatoes, chutney, mustard, and breadcrumbs together. Make 4 deep slits in each piece of chicken. Spread the devilled mixture over the top. Brush the foil with the oil. Place a chicken breast on each piece of foil. Drizzle any remaining oil over the top. Fold over the foil to make 4 loose parcels. Transfer to a baking sheet. Cook in the oven for 25 minutes. Open the foil parcels and cook for a further 5 minutes.

SERVES 4

CHICKEN CASSEROLE

This dish can either be cooked in the oven at 180°C (350°F/Gas mark 4) for 30 minutes, or on top of the stove.

45 ml (3 tbsp) OIL
1 LARGE ONION, CHOPPED
4 CHICKEN PORTIONS
55 g (2 oz) FLOUR
1 x 400 g (14 oz) CAN CHOPPED, PEELED TOMATOES
5 ml (1 tsp) MIXED DRIED HERBS

Heat the oil in a large pan. Fry the onion for 3 minutes. Coat the chicken portions in flour. Add the chicken to the pan and brown on both sides. Pour over the tomatoes. Fill the empty tomato can with water and pour into the pan. Stir in the herbs. Season. Cover and simmer for 30 minutes, adding a little extra boiling water if it simmers too rapidly, or transfer to a pre-heated oven.

SERVES 4

RIGHT: Devilled Chicken Baked in Foil

STUFFED PANCAKES

♨

8 PANCAKES, PRE-COOKED
25 g (1 oz) MARGARINE
25 g (1 oz) FLOUR
250 ml (½ scant pint) MILK
350 g (12 oz) COOKED CHICKEN, DICED
225 g (8 oz) TOMATOES, PEELED AND SLICED
55 g (2 oz) CHEDDAR CHEESE, GRATED

Pre-heat the oven to 200°C (400°F/Gas mark 6).

Warm the pancakes in the oven. Melt the margarine in a saucepan, then stir in the flour and cook for 2 minutes. Add the milk slowly, stirring constantly. Bring to the boil. Cool. Stir in the chicken.

Divide the mixture between the pancakes and roll up. Place in a greased ovenproof dish. Top with the tomatoes and cheese and bake for 30 minutes. SERVES 4

EGGS FLAMENCO

♨

30 ml (2 tbsp) OLIVE OIL
1 LARGE ONION, SLICED
2 cloves GARLIC, CHOPPED
225 g (8 oz) TOMATOES, PEELED AND SLICED
115 g (4 oz) CLOSED CUP MUSHROOMS, SLICED
2.5 ml (½ tsp) HOT PEPPER SAUCE
85 g (3 oz) COOKED PEAS
85 g (3 oz) GARLIC SAUSAGE, SLICED AND EACH
SLICE QUARTERED
115 g (4 oz) HAM, DICED
4 (size 4) EGGS
1 SMALL RED PEPPER, CHOPPED

Pre-heat the oven to 200°C (400°F/Gas Mark 6). Heat the oil in a saucepan and fry the onion and garlic until tender, but not brown. Add the tomatoes, mushrooms and hot pepper sauce and cook for 5 minutes. Add the peas, garlic sausage and ham, and heat thoroughly, stirring constantly. Turn into a shallow 23 cm (9 inch) ovenproof dish and spread the mixture to make it level. Make 4 slight indents with the back of a wooden spoon. Break the eggs over the top of the vegetable mixture and sprinkle with chopped red pepper. Bake for 10-15 minutes or until the whites of the eggs are set. SERVES 4

RIGHT: Eggs Flamenco

PESTO SAUCE

☙

Serve stirred into tomato-based pasta sauces.

45 g (1¹/₂ oz) BASIL, CHOPPED
2 cloves GARLIC, CRUSHED
55 g (2 oz) PINE NUTS, VERY FINELY CHOPPED
1 BEEF TOMATO, PEELED, SEEDED
AND FINELY CHOPPED
55 g (2 oz) PARMESAN CHEESE, GRATED
150 ml (5 fl oz) OLIVE OIL

Place the basil in a mortar and crush with the pestle. Add the garlic and pine nuts and pound again. Gradually add the tomato and cheese, pounding constantly until smooth. Transfer to a bowl and slowly beat in the olive oil, drop-by-drop, until the mixture becomes a smooth sauce. Store in an airtight container in the refrigerator. MAKES 450G (1 LB)

PASTA SAUCE

☙

Two sliced chillies or 5 ml (1 tsp) hot pepper sauce can be added to the tomatoes. Alternatively, add 15 ml (1 tbsp) capers or 6 black olives chopped with the oregano.

45 ml (3 tbsp) OLIVE OIL
1 RED ONION, FINELY CHOPPED
1 clove GARLIC, FINELY CHOPPED
1 kg (2 lbs) PLUM TOMATOES, PEELED AND CHOPPED
2 stems FRESH OREGANO
2.5 ml (¹/₂ tsp) SALT
1.25 ml (¹/₄ tsp) SUGAR
1.25 ml (¹/₄ tsp) BLACK PEPPER
5 ml (1 tsp) RED WINE VINEGAR

Heat the oil in a large pan. Fry the onion and garlic for 5 minutes. Add the tomatoes. Slowly bring to the boil. Cover and simmer for 8 minutes.

Strip the leaves from the oregano stems and chop the leaves. Add to the tomato sauce with salt, sugar, pepper and vinegar. Simmer for a further 2 minutes. Serve with cooked pasta. SERVES 4

TOP: Pesto Sauce
BOTTOM: Pasta Sauce

SPICY MACARONI CHEESE

🔥

30 ml (2 tbsp) OIL
1 LARGE ONION, FINELY CHOPPED
1 GREEN PEPPER, SEEDED AND CHOPPED
175 g (6 oz) BACON, CHOPPED
115 g (4 oz) CLOSED CUP MUSHROOMS, SLICED
1 x 400 g (14 oz) CAN CHOPPED PEELED TOMATOES
60 ml (4 tbsp) TOMATO PURÉE
30 ml (2 tbsp) WORCESTERSHIRE SAUCE
2.5 ml (1/2 tsp) CAYENNE PEPPER
1 x 200 g (7 oz) CAN SWEETCORN KERNELS, DRAINED
300 g (10 oz) MACARONI, COOKED AND DRAINED
115 g (4 oz) MATURE CHEDDAR CHEESE, GRATED
25 g (1 oz) DRIED BREADCRUMBS

Heat the oil and cook the onion and pepper until just soft. Add the bacon and cook for 2 minutes. Add the mushrooms and cook for a further minute. Stir in the tomatoes, tomato purée, Worcestershire sauce, cayenne, sweetcorn, and cooked macaroni, then cook over a gentle heat for 5 minutes. Stir in three quarters of the cheese. Turn into a warmed heatproof dish.

Pre-heat the grill. Quickly mix the remaining cheese and breadcrumbs together and sprinkle over the top of the macaroni mixture. Cook under the grill until the cheese has melted and turned golden brown. SERVES 4

FISH PIE

🔥

4 size 4 EGGS
700 g (1 1/2 lb) POTATOES
350 g (12 oz) COD OR HADDOCK FILLET, SKINNED AND DICED
350 g (12 oz) SMOKED COD OR HADDOCK FILLET, SKINNED AND DICED
1 LEEK, THINLY SLICED
175 g (6 oz) FROZEN PEAS, THAWED
150 ml (5 fl oz) PASSATA
450 g (1 lb) TOMATOES, PEELED AND SLICED
30 ml (2 tbsp) CHOPPED PARSLEY
85 g (3 oz) CHEDDAR CHEESE, GRATED
15 ml (1 tbsp) MILK (OPTIONAL)

Pre-heat the oven to 190°C (375°F/Gas mark 5). Hard boil the eggs for 10 minutes. Boil the potatoes until tender.

Meanwhile, put the fish in a greased 2.3 litre (4 pint) ovenproof casserole. Add the leek and peas and pour over the passata. Arrange a layer of sliced tomatoes on top. Shell the eggs, cut them into quarters and place on top of the tomatoes, yolks uppermost. Season and sprinkle over the parsley.

Mash the potatoes and beat in half the cheese, and a little milk if necessary, to make a creamy consistency. Use a piping bag with a large nozzle to pipe the potato in a lattice pattern on top of the pie. Sprinkle over the remaining grated cheese. Bake for 45-55 minutes.

SERVES 6

TOP: Spicy Macaroni Cheese
BOTTOM: Fish Pie

ROGAN JOSH

✤

This curry is best made the day before and reheated before serving.

2 LARGE ONIONS, CHOPPED

45 ml (3 tbsp) OIL

3 cloves GARLIC, CHOPPED

2-4 GREEN CHILLIES, SEEDED AND SLICED

1 bunch SPRING ONIONS, FINELY SLICED

1 kg (2 lb) STEWING LAMB, CUT INTO
2.5 CM (1 INCH) CUBES

20 ml (4 tsp) CUMIN

10 ml (2 tsp) CORIANDER

5 ml (1 tsp) TURMERIC

5 ml (1 tsp) CAYENNE PEPPER

1 kg (2 lb) TOMATOES, PEELED AND CHOPPED

115 g (4 oz) SPINACH, FINELY SHREDDED

To serve

30 ml (2 tbsp) OIL

450 g (1 lb) TOMATOES, QUARTERED

5 ml (1 tsp) CUMIN

350 g (12 oz) BASMATI RICE

Put the onions in a pan with 600 ml (1 pint) water. Bring to the boil and simmer for 1 hour until the onions are tender and the liquid has evaporated.

Pre-heat the oven to 160°C (325°F/Gas mark 3). Meanwhile, heat the oil in another pan and cook the garlic, chillies and spring onions for 5 minutes. Add the lamb and spices and brown the lamb thoroughly. Transfer to a casserole. Add the tomatoes and cooked onions. Stir well and season. Cover and cook in the oven for 1 3/4 hours.

Stir in the spinach and return to the oven. Cook for a further 1/4 hour or until the meat is tender.

To serve: heat the oil in a frying pan. Add the tomatoes and sprinkle over the cumin. Stir-fry for 15 minutes. Serve the tomatoes lightly mixed into the reheated curry. Serve with basmati rice.   SERVES 6

RIGHT: Rogan Josh

HUNGARIAN GOULASH

45 ml (3 tbsp) OIL

2 LARGE ONIONS, SLICED

2 cloves GARLIC, SLICED

30 ml (2 tbsp) FLOUR

20 ml (1½ tbsp) PAPRIKA

1 kg (2 lb) BONELESS PORK SHOULDER, CUBED

250 ml (9 fl oz) RED WINE

1 x 400 g (14 oz) CAN CHOPPED, PEELED TOMATOES

1 LARGE GREEN PEPPER, SEEDED
AND SLICED

5 ml (1 tsp) DRIED THYME

2 BAY LEAVES

225 g (8 oz) CLOSED CUP MUSHROOMS, SLICED

Pre-heat the oven to 160°C (325°F/Gas mark 3). Heat 30 ml (2 tbsp) of the oil in a large pan and gently fry the onions and garlic for 5 minutes. Meanwhile, mix the flour and paprika together and coat the pork with this mixture. Transfer the onions and garlic to a casserole. Add the remaining oil to the pan, then cook the pork briskly for 5 minutes to brown well. Transfer to the casserole. Add the wine, tomatoes, green pepper and herbs. Season. Cover and cook in the oven for 1½ hours.

Add the mushrooms and cook for a further 15 minutes or until the pork is tender. SERVES 6

STIFADO

90 ml (6 tbsp) OIL

1 kg (2 lbs) ONIONS, CHOPPED

4 cloves GARLIC, CHOPPED

1 kg (2 lbs) STEWING BEEF, CUT INTO
2.5 CM (1 INCH) CUBES

1 kg (2 lbs) PLUM TOMATOES, PEELED AND CHOPPED

45 ml (3 tbsp) TOMATO PURÉE

200 ml (7 fl oz) RED WINE

Pre-heat the oven to 150°C (300°F/Gas mark 2). Heat 60 ml (4 tbsp) of the oil in a large pan. Gently cook the onions and garlic for 15 minutes until tender and reduced by half. Transfer to a 2.3 litre (4 pint) ovenproof casserole. Heat the remaining oil in pan and brown the beef. Transfer to the casserole and add the tomatoes and tomato purée. Stir well. Pour over the wine. Season. Cover with a tight fitting lid. Cook in the oven for 5 hours until the meat is tender and the sauce reduced to resemble the consistency of jam. SERVES 6-8

TOP: *Hungarian Goulash*

BOTTOM: *Stifado*

TEXAN CHICKEN

If using a turkey, instead of a chicken, double the quantity of the other ingredients.

1.4 kg (3 lb) FRESH CHICKEN

Sauce

30 ml (2 tbsp) TOMATO PURÉE

15 ml (1 tbsp) RED WINE VINEGAR

5 ml (1 tsp) CASTER SUGAR

2.5 ml (½ tsp) WORCESTERSHIRE SAUCE

1.25 ml (¼ tsp) HOT PEPPER SAUCE

5 ml (1 tsp) PAPRIKA

2.5 ml (½ tsp) CHILLI POWDER

1.25 ml (¼ tsp) GROUND BLACK PEPPER

1.25 ml (¼ tsp) SALT

1 clove GARLIC, CRUSHED

5 ml (1 tsp) OIL

5 ml (1 tsp) PAPRIKA

450 g (1 lb) TOMATOES, HALVED

Gently ease the skin away from the chicken breast, being careful not to break the skin. Mix the sauce ingredients together and spoon the mixture under the skin, easing it along the whole breast. Refrigerate for 6 hours to allow the sauce to flavour the chicken.

Pre-heat the oven to 190°C (375°F/Gas mark 5). Rub the chicken all over with oil and paprika. Transfer to a roasting tin. Roast for 1 hour.

Remove from the oven and drain off excess fat from the roasting tin. Arrange the tomatoes, cut side up, around the chicken. Baste the tomatoes with juices in the roasting tin. Return to oven and cook for a further 20 minutes. Lift the chicken and tomatoes out of the roasting tin. Use the juices in the roasting tin to make the gravy.

SERVES 4

FISH CREOLE

juice 2 LIMES

700 g (1½ lb) HOKI OR COD FILLET, SKINNED AND CUT INTO CHUNKS

2 cloves GARLIC

8 SPRING ONIONS, CHOPPED

30 ml (2 tbsp) OIL

2 GREEN CHILLIES, SEEDED AND THINLY SLICED

700 g (1½ lb) TOMATOES, PEELED AND SLICED

6 DRIED SUN-DRIED TOMATOES, SOAKED AND CHOPPED

150 ml (5 fl oz) WHITE WINE

1.25-2.5 ml (¼-½ tsp) HOT PEPPER SAUCE

55 g (2 oz) FLOUR

GREEN SALAD, TO SERVE

Pre-heat the oven to 200°C (400°F/Gas mark 6). Pour the lime juice over the fish. Marinate for 20 minutes.

Meanwhile, fry the garlic and spring onions in half the oil. Add the chillies, fresh and dried tomatoes and simmer for 10 minutes. Add the wine and simmer for a further 5 minutes. Transfer to a shallow ovenproof dish. Season with the hot pepper sauce. Set aside. Strain the marinade and pat the fish dry on kitchen paper. Coat the fish in flour and fry gently in the remaining oil until golden brown but not cooked through. Lay the fish on top of the tomatoes. Cover and cook for 10 minutes.

SERVES 4

RIGHT: Fish Creole

ENTERTAINING

Greet guests with a cocktail and pass round tomatoes stuffed with quails eggs. For a main course try Veal Parmigiana, Spiced Sirloin Steak or Tomato Soufflé. Many tomato dishes can be prepared in advance, avoiding a last-minute panic before friends or family arrive.

BLOODY MARY

2 ICE CUBES
2 *measures* VODKA
115 *ml (4 fl oz)* TOMATO JUICE
few drops LEMON JUICE
CELERY SALT
few drops HOT PEPPER SAUCE
few drops WORCESTERSHIRE SAUCE
few drops SHERRY
FRESHLY GROUND PEPPER

Place all the ingredients in a jug and mix well with a fork. Pour into a glass. SERVES 1

CHEESE AND TOMATO D'ARTOIS

450 *g (1 lb)* PACKET FROZEN PUFF PASTRY, DEFROSTED

Filling
25 *g (1 oz)* BUTTER
450 *g (1 lb)* TOMATOES, PEELED, SEEDED
AND CHOPPED
1 x 50 *g (1³/4 oz)* CAN ANCHOVY FILLETS, DRAINED
AND CHOPPED
225 *g (8 oz)* CHEDDAR CHEESE, GRATED
1 *size 2* EGG
pinch CAYENNE PEPPER
little MILK, TO GLAZE
SESAME SEEDS

Pre-heat the oven to 220°C (425°F/Gas mark 7). Roll out the pastry into a rectangle approximately 30 x 35 cm (12 inches x 16 inches). Cut lengthways to give 4 pieces of pastry 30 x 10 cm (12 inches x 4 inches) long. Place 2 pieces on a large baking tray that has been wetted.

To make the filling, cream the butter, add the tomatoes, anchovies, cheese, egg and cayenne to taste. Mix well, and spread over the pastry on the baking tray. Damp the edges and cover with remaining pastry. Seal the edges well. Glaze the top with a little milk and sprinkle with sesame seeds. Bake for about 25 minutes, or until golden, changing shelf positions about half way through the cooking. Cool until cold. Cut into 2.5 cm (1 inch) fingers. Serve warm. MAKES 24

TOP: Bloody Mary
BOTTOM: Cheese and Tomato D'Artois

STILTON-STUFFED CHERRY TOMATOES

350 g (12 oz) CHERRY TOMATOES
115 g (4 oz) STILTON CHEESE
75 ml (5 tbsp) CRÈME FRAÎCHE

Slice the tops off the tomatoes. Use a sharp knife to remove the core and seeds. Place the tomatoes upside down to drain.

Break the stilton down with a fork into small crumbs, then blend in the crème fraîche. Cut a very small slice off the base of each tomato. Use a piping bag with a star nozzle, to pipe the stilton mixture into each tomato.

MAKES ABOUT 30

QUAILS EGGS IN TOMATO NESTS

12 QUAILS EGGS
225 g (8 oz) COCKTAIL TOMATOES
5 ml (1 tsp) CAYENNE PEPPER

Place the eggs in a pan of cold water and slowly bring to the boil. Simmer for 3 minutes. Plunge into cold water.

Halve the tomatoes and remove cores and seeds. Place the tomatoes upside down to drain. Shell the eggs and cut each egg in half. Cut a very small slice off the base of each half tomato. Fill each half tomato with halved eggs. Sprinkle with cayenne.

MAKES 24

TOP: *Stilton-stuffed Tomatoes*
BOTTOM: *Quails Eggs in Tomato Nests*

POACHED QUAIL WITH MADEIRA SAUCE

Sauce

450 g (1 lb) TOMATOES, PEELED, SEEDED
AND CHOPPED

1 clove GARLIC, CRUSHED

30 ml (2 tbsp) OLIVE OIL

sprig PARSLEY

Stock

300 ml (¹/₂ pint) FRESH CHICKEN STOCK

1 ONION, CHOPPED

1 CARROT, CHOPPED

1 BAY LEAF

8 x 115 g (4 oz) QUAILS

25 g (1 oz) FLOUR

25 g (1 oz) BUTTER

15 ml (1 tbsp) OLIVE OIL

8 rounds WHITE BREAD

30 ml (2 tbsp) MADEIRA

To make the sauce, put the tomatoes in a saucepan with the garlic, oil and parsley. Season. Cover and simmer for 30 minutes.

Remove the parsley sprig from the tomatoes and strain the tomato sauce through a nylon sieve into a bowl. Keep warm.

Meanwhile, pour the chicken stock into another saucepan, add the onion, carrot and bay leaf. Bring to the boil and simmer for 20 minutes.

Dust the quails with flour. Heat the butter and oil in a frying pan and gently brown the quails, turning regularly, for 10 minutes. Strain off any excess fat. Turn the quails on their sides. Strain the stock into the frying pan. Cover and cook very slowly for 10 minutes. Turn the quails to cook on the other side for a further 5 minutes. Pierce with a sharp knife; the juices should be clear.

Toast the bread. Remove trussing strings from the quails. Place the toast on a warm serving dish and top with the cooked quails. Reduce the stock in a frying pan by boiling fast, uncovered, until there is about 85 ml (3 fl oz). Add the prepared tomato sauce. Stir in the Madeira. Strain the sauce and serve. SERVES 4

RIGHT: Poached Quail with Madeira Sauce

SPICED ROAST BEEF WITH TOMATO AND GINGER SAUCE

Marinade

30 ml (2 tbsp) TOMATO PURÉE

15 ml (1 tbsp) RED WINE VINEGAR

60 ml (4 tbsp) OIL

15 ml (1 tbsp) DEMERARA SUGAR

1 clove GARLIC, CRUSHED

7.5 ml (1½ tsp) GRATED FRESH ROOT GINGER

2.5 ml (½ tsp) SALT

900 g (2 lb) FILLET OF BEEF

15 ml (1 tbsp) MIXED (GREEN, RED, BLACK, WHITE) PEPPERCORNS, CRUSHED

300 ml (10 fl oz) NATURAL FROMAGE FRAIS

To serve

LOLLO BIONDO LETTUCE

CORN SALAD LEAVES

CHERRY TOMATOES

Mix all the ingredients for the marinade together. Spread over the beef. Sprinkle the crushed peppercorns over the top and lightly press into the beef. Cover, then leave to marinate overnight.

Preheat the oven to 240°C (475°F/Gas mark 9). Transfer the beef and juices to a small roasting tin. Roast for 20 minutes, basting occasionally. Reduce the oven temperature to 220°C (425°F/Gas mark 7), and cook for a further 20 minutes for medium beef or 25 minutes for well done. Remove from the roasting tin and leave to cool completely. Strain and reserve juices.

When cool, make a sauce by stirring the juices into the fromage frais. Check the seasoning. With a very sharp knife, cut the beef into very thin slices. Arrange on a platter with the salad leaves and tomatoes. Serve with the sauce.

SERVES 6

CHICKEN WITH PASSATA MAYONNAISE

Mayonnaise

3 (size 3) EGG YOLKS

7.5 ml (1½ tsp) CASTER SUGAR

5 ml (1 tsp) ANCHOVY PASTE

5 ml (1 tsp) POWDERED MUSTARD

1.25 ml (¼ tsp) BLACK PEPPER

45 ml (3 tbsp) TARRAGON VINEGAR

225 ml (8 fl oz) EXTRA VIRGIN OLIVE OIL

115 ml (4 fl oz) PASSATA

8 CHICKEN PORTIONS, COOKED AND SKINNED

4 SPRING ONIONS, FINELY SLICED

SLICED TOMATOES, TO SERVE

Place all the mayonnaise ingredients, except the oil and passata, in a blender or food processor. Blend, then add the oil, a few drops at a time and blend well. Continue to add oil through the feed tube in a steady stream, blending well until the mayonnaise is a thick spooning consistency. Stir in the passata. Arrange the chicken portions on a serving platter and spoon over the tomato mayonnaise. Sprinkle over the spring onions. Serve with sliced tomatoes.

SERVES 8

Top: Tomato and Garlic Mini Rolls (see page 40)

Bottom: Spiced Roast Beef with Tomato and Ginger Sauce

ROSEMARY BAKED MACKEREL

1 SMALL ONION, THINLY SLICED
1 MEDIUM SIZED APPLE, CORED AND THINLY SLICED
225 g (8 oz) TOMATOES, PEELED AND CHOPPED
280 ml (scant 1/2 pint) FISH OR CHICKEN STOCK
small sprig ROSEMARY
dash WORCESTERSHIRE SAUCE
4 x 175-225 g (6-8 oz) MACKEREL FILLETS

Pre-heat the oven to 190°C (375°F/Gas Mark 5). Place the onion, apple, tomatoes and stock in a saucepan. Add the rosemary and Worcestershire sauce. Season. Bring to the boil, cover and cook for 10 minutes.

Fold the mackerel fillets in half with the skin side outermost and place in an ovenproof dish. Pour the sauce over the fish. Cover with foil and bake for 20-25 minutes.

SERVES 4

LEMON SOLE EN PAPILLOTE

This recipe also works well with plaice fillets

8 x 115 g (4 oz) LEMON SOLE FILLETS

Stuffing
175 g (6 oz) CHERRY TOMATOES, SLICED
1 ONION, FINELY CHOPPED
85 g (3 oz) FRESH WHITE BREADCRUMBS
juice 1 LEMON
1 (size 3) EGG YOLK
4 sprigs DILL, CHOPPED

sprigs DILL, TO GARNISH

Pre-heat the oven to 190°C (375°F/Gas mark 5). Skin the fish fillets. Mix all the stuffing ingredients together. Place a spoonful on each fish fillet and roll up, securing the end of the fillet underneath with a wooden cocktail stick.

Cut 4 pieces of greaseproof paper 38 cm (15 inches) square. Place 2 fish fillets on one side of the greaseproof paper. Fold over the other side of the paper, covering the fish. Pleat the edges of the paper together to make a parcel. Repeat with remaining parcels. Place on a baking sheet and cook in the oven for 15 minutes. Open the parcels, transfer the fish to serving plates, garnish and serve immediately.

SERVES 4

RIGHT: Rosemary Baked Mackerel

VEAL PARMIGIANA

Double the quantities for a dinner party main course.

4 x 85 g (3 oz) VEAL ESCALOPES
1 (size 3) EGG, BEATEN
85 g (3 oz) FRESH WHITE BREADCRUMBS
55 g (2 oz) PARMESAN CHEESE, GRATED
60 ml (4 tbsp) OLIVE OIL
1 ONION, CHOPPED
1 clove GARLIC, CHOPPED
700 g (1½ lb) TOMATOES, PEELED AND CHOPPED
15 ml (1 tbsp) TOMATO PURÉE
5 ml (1 tsp) FRESH THYME LEAVES
4 BASIL LEAVES, CHOPPED
55 g (2 oz) BUTTER
150 g (5 oz) MOZZARELLA CHEESE, SLICED
sprigs BASIL, TO GARNISH

Pre-heat the oven to 180°C (350°F/Gas mark 4). Dip the veal escalopes in the beaten egg. Mix the breadcrumbs with half the Parmesan cheese and coat the veal. Set aside. Heat half the oil in a frying pan and fry the onion and garlic for 3 minutes. Add the tomatoes, tomato purée, thyme, and basil. Season. Slowly bring to the boil, cover and simmer for 10 minutes. Transfer the tomato mixture to a shallow ovenproof dish.

Heat the remaining oil and the butter in a frying pan and fry the escalopes quickly until golden brown on both sides. Arrange the escalopes and mozzarella in alternate overlapping slices on top of the tomato mixture. Sprinkle over the remaining Parmesan. Bake uncovered, for 15 minutes. Garnish with basil. SERVES 4

SPICED SIRLOIN STEAK

5 ml (1 tsp) OIL
4 x 150 g (5 oz) SIRLOIN STEAKS
2 LARGE BEEF TOMATOES, SLICED
225 g (8 oz) OPEN CUP MUSHROOMS
2 GREEN CHILLIES, SEEDED AND SLICED
10 ml (2 tsp) FRESH THYME
4 BAY LEAVES
225 ml (8 fl oz) RED WINE
10 ml (2 tsp) CORNFLOUR

Pre-heat the oven to 180°C (350°F/Gas mark 4). Heat the oil in a frying pan and quickly brown the steaks on both sides. Transfer to a large, shallow casserole. Top with the sliced tomatoes and mushrooms, cap side uppermost. Sprinkle over the chillies, thyme and bay leaves. Pour over the wine. Cover and cook in the oven for 30 minutes.

Gently lift the steaks, tomatoes and mushrooms from the casserole. Transfer to a serving dish. Boil the wine mixture to reduce it by about a third. Mix the cornflour with a little cold water and stir the mixture into the wine. Return to the boil. Strain, pour over steaks and serve with a green salad. SERVES 4

RIGHT: Veal Parmigiana

TOMATO AND CHEESE ROULADE

🍅

15 g (½ oz) BUTTER
450 g (1 lb) TOMATOES, PEELED AND FINELY CHOPPED
25 g (1 oz) WHOLEMEAL FLOUR
3 (size 3) EGGS, SEPARATED
1 (size 3) EGG WHITE

Filling
55 g (2 oz) CHEDDAR CHEESE, GRATED
30 ml (2 tbsp) TOMATO CHUTNEY
2.5 ml (½ tsp) MADE MUSTARD
30 ml (2 tbsp) CHOPPED WATERCRESS

RADICCHIO AND TARRAGON, TO SERVE

Pre-heat the oven to 190°C (375°F/Gas mark 5). Lightly grease a Swiss roll tin, approximately 30 cm by 20 cm (12 inches x 8 inches) and line it with baking parchment. Melt the butter in a pan, add the tomatoes and cook for about 4 minutes until pulpy. Stir in the flour and cook over a gentle heat for 1 minute. Remove the pan from the heat. Season. Beat in the egg yolks. Whisk the egg whites until stiff, but not dry, and fold lightly, but thoroughly, into the tomato mixture. Spread evenly into the prepared tin, making sure that the mixture reaches right to the edges. Bake for about 20 minutes until just set and firm to the touch.

Meanwhile, make the filling. Mix three quarters of the grated cheese with the chutney, mustard and half the watercress. Season. Quickly turn the cooked roulade out onto a clean sheet of baking parchment; remove the lining paper. Spread the filling evenly over the roulade and roll up like a Swiss roll. Place on an ovenproof serving dish and sprinkle with the remaining watercress and cheese. Return to the oven for 2-3 minutes. Serve sliced, with radicchio and tarragon. SERVES 4

TOMATO SOUFFLÉ

🍅

To make the white sauce for this recipe, follow the instructions on page 52 (Stuffed Pancakes).

25 g (1 oz) MARGARINE
25 g (1 oz) FLOUR
150 ml (¼ pint) MILK
1 x 500 g (18 oz) CARTON CREAMED TOMATOES OR
500 ml (18 fl oz) PASSATA
4 (size 4) EGGS, SEPARATED
1 (size 4) EGG WHITE
3 TOMATOES, PEELED, SEEDED AND FINELY CHOPPED

Pre-heat the oven to 200°C (400°F/Gas mark 6). Make a thick white sauce. Remove from the heat and stir in the creamed tomatoes and egg yolks. Whisk all the egg whites until stiff. Stir the chopped tomatoes into the creamed tomato mixture, then gently fold in the beaten egg whites. Pour into a greased 2.3 litre (4 pint) soufflé dish. Cook in the oven for 40 minutes. Serve immediately. SERVES 5

RIGHT: Tomato and Cheese Roulade

VEGETARIAN DISHES

Many families now regularly cater for one or more vegetarian, and meatless meals are increasing in popularity. Tomatoes contribute to countless vegetable-based dishes, which can be enjoyed by vegetarians and meat-eaters alike.

VEGETABLE MOUSSAKA

1 LARGE AUBERGINE
3 LARGE POTATOES, PEELED AND SLICED
90 ml (6 tbsp) OIL
1 LARGE ONION, SLICED
1 kg (2 lb) TOMATOES, PEELED AND SLICED
225 g (8 oz) CLOSED CUP MUSHROOMS, SLICED
2 LARGE COURGETTES, THINLY SLICED
1 RED PEPPER, SEEDED AND THINLY SLICED
25 g (1 oz) MARGARINE
25 g (1 oz) FLOUR
300 ml (1/2 pint) MILK
1 (size 3) EGG YOLK
55 g (2 oz) COARSELY GRATED PARMESAN CHEESE
GREEN SALAD, TO SERVE

Slice the aubergine and sprinkle the slices with salt. Leave for 1/2 hour, then drain. Pre-heat the oven to 180°C (350°F/Gas mark 4).

Meanwhile, heat 45 ml (3 tbsp) oil in a large frying pan and gently fry the potatoes on both sides for 5 minutes, until golden brown. Transfer to a plate and keep warm. Pour the remaining oil into the pan and fry the onion until tender. Add the drained aubergine slices and fry for 5 minutes. Add the tomatoes and cook for a further 5 minutes.

Lightly grease a 2.3 litre (4 pint) casserole dish. Line the dish with half the potatoes. Add half the tomato and aubergine mixture, followed by a layer of mushrooms, courgettes and red pepper, seasoning each layer. Add the remaining tomato and aubergine mixture and top with the remaining potatoes. Make a white sauce by melting the margarine in a small pan. Stir in the flour and cook for 1 minute. Remove from the heat and gradually stir in the milk. Return to the heat and bring to the boil, stirring constantly. Cool slightly, then stir in the egg yolk. Spread the white sauce over the potatoes and sprinkle on the cheese. Cover and cook in the oven for 1 hour. Remove the lid and cook for a further 1/2 hour. Serve with salad. SERVES 6

RIGHT: *Vegetable Moussaka*

TOMATO RISOTTO

45 ml (3 tbsp) OLIVE OIL

1 ONION, FINELY CHOPPED

1 clove GARLIC, CHOPPED

250 g (9 oz) RISOTTO RICE

900 ml (1½ pints) HOT VEGETABLE STOCK

1 x 175 ml (6 fl oz) CAN TOMATO JUICE

225 g (8 oz) TOMATOES, PEELED AND SEEDED

3 SUN-DRIED TOMATOES IN OIL,
DRAINED AND CHOPPED

6 LARGE BASIL LEAVES, CHOPPED

85 g (3 oz) MOZZARELLA CHEESE, FINELY CHOPPED

Heat the oil in a large saucepan. Add onion and garlic and fry until soft. Add the rice and stir over a low heat for 2 minutes. Add 300 ml (½ pint) of the stock and cook gently, stirring until the liquid has been absorbed, then add another 300 ml (½ pint) of stock. Repeat as before.

Meanwhile, add the tomato juice to the remaining stock and reheat to simmering point. Add the stock and tomato juice to the risotto, together with the fresh and sun-dried tomatoes. Cook, stirring, until the liquid has been absorbed and the rice is tender. Remove from the heat and stir in the basil. Stir in the cheese and serve immediately.

SERVES 3

BOSTON BEANS

225 g (8 oz) DRIED HARICOT BEANS,
SOAKED OVERNIGHT

1 LARGE RED SPANISH ONION, SLICED

190 ml (6½ fl oz) TOMATO JUICE

300 ml (½ pint) VEGETABLE STOCK

15 ml (1 tbsp) BLACK TREACLE

15 ml (1 tbsp) WHOLE GRAIN MUSTARD

30 ml (2 tbsp) TOMATO PURÉE

225 g (8 oz) TOMATOES, QUARTERED

225 g (8 oz) CLOSED CUP MUSHROOMS

Drain the haricot beans, transfer to a saucepan with the onion, tomato juice, stock, black treacle, mustard and tomato purée. Bring to the boil, cover and cook for 10 minutes. Reduce the heat and cook gently for 1 hour 40 minutes.

Stir in the tomatoes and mushrooms, cover and continue cooking for about 45 minutes, or until the beans are soft.

SERVES 4

TOP: Tomato Risotto
BOTTOM: Boston Beans

TOMATO AND COURGETTE LAYER

☙

30 ml (2 tbsp) OIL

15 g (½ oz) BUTTER

1 SMALL ONION, CHOPPED

350 g (12 oz) TOMATOES, PEELED AND SLICED

700 g (1½ lb) COURGETTES, CUT INTO 1 CM (½ INCH) THICK SLICES

45 g (1½ oz) MARGARINE

45 g (1½ oz) FLOUR

425 ml (¾ pint) MILK

115 g (4 oz) CHEDDAR CHEESE, GRATED

15 ml (1 tbsp) BREADCRUMBS

Pre-heat the oven to 190°C (375°F/Gas mark 5). Heat the oil and butter in a pan and fry the onion until soft but not browned. Add the tomatoes and fry for 5 minutes. Arrange a layer of courgettes in a greased ovenproof casserole dish followed by a layer of tomatoes. Continue with layers, seasoning with salt and pepper between each layer. Cover and bake for 1 hour until tender.

Meanwhile, make a white sauce following the method on page 78. Stir in half the cheese. Drain off the liquid and mix it with the cheese sauce until it is of a coating consistency. Pour over the vegetables. Mix the remaining grated cheese and breadcrumbs together and sprinkle over the top. Place under a hot grill, or return to the oven, until golden brown and bubbling. Serve immediately.

SERVES 4

TOMATO AND COURGETTE FLAN

☙

175 g (6 oz) SHORTCRUST PASTRY

450 g (1 lb) TOMATOES, PEELED AND SLICED

225 g (8 oz) COURGETTES, SLICED AND BLANCHED

2 (size 3) EGGS

1 x 150 ml (5 fl oz) carton SINGLE CREAM

15 ml (1 tbsp) FRESHLY CHOPPED PARSLEY

5 ml (1 tsp) FRESHLY CHOPPED CHIVES

5 ml (1 tsp) FRESHLY CHOPPED SAGE

sprig PARSLEY, TO GARNISH

Pre-heat the oven to 220°C (425°F/Gas mark 7). Roll out the pastry thinly and line a 20 cm (8 inch) flan tin with it. Line the pastry case with greaseproof paper and baking beans and bake blind for 15-20 minutes. Reduce the oven temperature to 190°C (375°F/Gas mark 5).

Remove the greaseproof paper and baking beans. Arrange the tomatoes and courgettes in the par-baked pastry case. Beat the eggs, cream, parsley, chives and sage together. Season. Pour into the pastry case. Bake for about 30-40 minutes, until the filling is lightly set. Garnish with parsley. Serve warm.

SERVES 4-6

RIGHT: Tomato and Courgette Flan

TOMATO AND LEEK CROUSTADES

This mixture also fills a 20 cm (8 inch) flan. Increase the cooking time to 15 minutes to bake the flan and to 12 minutes for the filling.

115 g (4 oz) FRESH WHOLEMEAL BREADCRUMBS
100 g (3½ oz) GROUND ALMONDS
115 g (4 oz) MARGARINE

Filling
25 g (1 oz) MARGARINE
175 g (6 oz) LEEKS, SLICED
15 ml (1 tbsp) FLOUR
200 ml (7 fl oz) CRÈME FRAÎCHE
225 g (8 oz) TOMATOES, PEELED AND SLICED
55 g (2 oz) CHEDDAR CHEESE, GRATED

Pre-heat the oven to 190°C (375°F/Gas Mark 5). Mix the breadcrumbs, almonds and margarine together. Use to line 5, 10 cm (4 inch) loose-bottomed flan tins. Bake for 10 minutes.

Meanwhile, melt the margarine in a pan and cook the leeks for 5 minutes. Stir in the flour and cook for 1 minute. Stir in the crème fraîche and bring slowly to the boil to thicken. Spoon into the flan cases. Top with the sliced tomatoes and sprinkle over the cheese. Return to the oven and cook for a further 10 minutes. Serve hot or cold.

MAKES 5

FRESH TOMATO TART

175 g (6 oz) WHOLEMEAL SHORTCRUST PASTRY
15 ml (1 tbsp) OLIVE OIL
700 g (1½ lb) TOMATOES, PEELED, SEEDED
  AND CHOPPED
1 large clove GARLIC, PEELED AND CRUSHED
45 ml (3 tbsp) TOMATO PURÉE
2.5 ml (½ tsp) GRATED ORANGE RIND
5 ml (1 tsp) CHOPPED FRESH MINT
2.5 ml (½ tsp) BROWN SUGAR
85 g (3 oz) MOZZARELLA CHEESE, THINLY SLICED
sprig BASIL, TO GARNISH

Pre-heat the oven to 190°C (375°F/Gas mark 5). Roll out the pastry thinly and line a 20 cm (8 inch) flan tin with it. Line the pastry case with greaseproof paper and baking beans. Bake blind for 10 minutes.

Meanwhile, prepare the filling. Heat the oil in a large pan. Add the tomatoes and garlic. Cook gently for 5 minutes. Add the tomato purée, orange rind, mint and sugar. Cook gently for 10-15 minutes until the sauce is thick and richly coloured. Season. Remove the greaseproof paper and baking beans from the pastry case. Spread the tomato mixture evenly in the par-baked pastry case. Top with the slices of cheese. Return to the oven for 30 minutes. Serve warm, cut into wedges and garnish with basil.

SERVES 4-6

RIGHT: Tomato and Leek Croustades

RATATOUILLE

45 ml (3 tbsp) OLIVE OIL
2 ONIONS, SLICED
2 cloves GARLIC, FINELY CHOPPED
1 LARGE AUBERGINE, CHOPPED
450 g (1 lb) TOMATOES, QUARTERED
3 COURGETTES, SLICED
1 GREEN PEPPER, SEEDED AND CHOPPED
30 ml (2 tbsp) MIXED FRESH HERBS, CHOPPED
30 ml (2 tbsp) TOMATO PURÉE

Slice the aubergine and sprinkle slices with salt. Leave for $^1/_2$ hour, then drain. Heat the oil and fry the onions and garlic for 2 minutes. Add the aubergine and fry for 5 minutes. Add the tomatoes, courgettes, pepper and herbs. Cook very gently for 15 minutes, stirring occasionally. Stir in the tomato purée and season.

SERVES 6

BAKED TOMATOES

These tomatoes are filled with Pesto Sauce (see page 54) and baked in a conventional oven or cooked in a microwave.
8 TOMATOES
75 ml (5 tbsp) PESTO SAUCE (SEE PAGE 54)

Halve the tomatoes. Scoop out the seeds and flesh. Stand upside down to drain for 10 minutes. Spoon some pesto into each tomato half.

To microwave: arrange the tomato halves on a plate. Cover with microwave film and cook on full power for 3 $^1/_2$ minutes.

To bake: pre-heat the oven to 180°C (350°F/Gas mark 4) and bake for 10 minutes. Serve as a vegetable accompaniment.

SERVES 4

RIGHT: Ratatouille

GRILLED TOMATOES

450 g (1 lb) TOMATOES, HALVED
25 g (1 oz) BUTTER, MELTED
45 g (1½ oz) FRESH WHITE BREADCRUMBS (OPTIONAL)
15 ml (1 tbsp) CHOPPED CHIVES (OPTIONAL)
25 g (1 oz) GRATED PARMESAN CHEESE (OPTIONAL)

For plain grilled tomatoes, brush the tomatoes with melted butter and season. Or, mix the breadcrumbs with melted butter. Sprinkle over the tomatoes and season.

Alternatively, mix breadcrumbs with melted butter and chives. Sprinkle over the tomatoes and season.

For a cheesy topping, mix the breadcrumbs with melted butter and Parmesan. Sprinkle over the tomatoes and season.

For any of the above, place the tomatoes, cut side up, on a grill pan. Fix the grill pan on a low rack and grill under a medium heat for 3 minutes. Cook slowly to avoid the tops burning before the tomatoes are heated through.

SERVES 4

TOMATOES AND COURGETTES

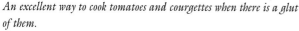

An excellent way to cook tomatoes and courgettes when there is a glut of them.

45 ml (3 tbsp) OLIVE OIL
700 g (1½ lbs) COURGETTES, SLICED
450 g (1 lb) TOMATOES, PEELED AND QUARTERED
4 BASIL LEAVES, CHOPPED

Heat the oil in a pan. Fry the courgettes briskly for 10 minutes, until golden brown. Lower the heat, add the tomatoes. Cover and cook gently for 10 minutes.

Stir in the basil and season well. Serve immediately as a vegetable or cool, transfer to freezer bags, label and freeze.

SERVES 6

RIGHT: Grilled Tomatoes

MARINADES, CHUTNEYS AND RELISHES

Late summer is the time to make tomato chutneys, pickles and relishes. The recipes here have been created with the *Sandwiches and Snacks* chapter in mind. Tomatoes add colour as well as flavour to marinades for barbecued meat, poultry or fish.

PIQUANT TOMATO MARINADE

For a barbecue, this quantity will marinate 8 chicken drumsticks.

60 ml (4 tbsp) CLEAR HONEY
30 ml (2 tbsp) TOMATO PURÉE
30 ml (2 tbsp) MALT VINEGAR
30 ml (2 tbsp) SOY SAUCE
5 ml (1 tsp) GROUND GINGER
3 drops HOT PEPPER SAUCE

Gently warm the honey in a saucepan or in the microwave on medium for 30 seconds. Stir in the remaining ingredients. Use to marinate chicken drumsticks for 6 hours prior to cooking on the barbecue.

TOMATO, ORANGE AND LEMON MARINADE

For a barbecue, this quantity will marinate 20 pork spare ribs.

60 ml (4 tbsp) CLEAR HONEY
45 ml (3 tbsp) TOMATO PURÉE
45 ml (3 tbsp) SOY SAUCE
5 ml (1 tsp) DIJON MUSTARD
1 clove GARLIC, CRUSHED
45 ml (3 tbsp) ORANGE JUICE
45 ml (3 tbsp) LEMON JUICE

Gently warm the honey gently in a saucepan or in the microwave on medium for 30 seconds. Stir in the remaining ingredients. Use to marinate spare ribs for 6 hours prior to cooking on the barbecue.

TOMATO GLAZE

For cooking meat, poultry or fish on a barbecue.

30 ml (2 tbsp) TOMATO PURÉE
15 ml (1 tbsp) SOY SAUCE
15 ml (1 tbsp) OIL

Brush the meat, poultry or fish with the tomato glaze every 5 minutes while the food is cooking on the barbecue.

FROM LEFT TO RIGHT: Piquant Tomato Marinade, Tomato, Orange and Lemon Marinade, Tomato Glaze

GREEN TOMATO CHUTNEY

450 g (1 lb) ONIONS, CHOPPED

25 g (1 oz) PICKLING SPICE

2.25 kg (5 lb) GREEN TOMATOES, PEELED
AND QUARTERED

10 ml (2 tsp) SALT

550 ml (20 fl oz) MALT VINEGAR

450 g (1 lb) GRANULATED SUGAR

Put the onions and 150 ml (¹/₄ pint) water in a large saucepan and cook until soft. Drain off the water. Tie the pickling spice in a muslin bag. Tie firmly to the saucepan handle with the bag inside the pan. Add the tomatoes and salt and bring to the boil. Reduce the heat and simmer for 1 hour, stirring occasionally.

When the mixture thickens add a little of the malt vinegar. Finally add the remaining malt vinegar and the sugar to the saucepan and cook until the mixture is thick, stirring frequently. When the chutney is ready, remove the muslin bag. Pour the chutney into sterilised hot jars and seal. Store for 1 month before using. Best consumed within 6 months. MAKES 1.4 KG (3 LBS)

RIPE TOMATO CHUTNEY

550 ml (20 fl oz) MALT VINEGAR

15 g (¹/₂ oz) PICKLING SPICE

2.75 kg (6 lbs) RIPE TOMATOES, PEELED AND QUARTERED

2 LARGE ONIONS, CHOPPED

10 ml (2 tsp) PAPRIKA

1.25 ml (¹/₄ tsp) CAYENNE PEPPER

15 ml (1 tbsp) SALT

350 g (12 oz) GRANULATED SUGAR

Make a medium-spiced vinegar by boiling the pickling spice in the vinegar for 10 minutes. Cool. The spices may be left in the cooling vinegar if desired, to increase the spicing.

Put the tomatoes in a large saucepan with the chopped onions. Heat gently, then simmer to a thick pulp, stirring occasionally. Add half the strained spiced vinegar together with the paprika and cayenne. Sprinkle over the salt and bring to the boil. Cook, uncovered, until thickened.

Meanwhile, heat the remaining strained, spiced vinegar with the sugar until dissolved. Add to the tomatoes. Boil and reduce to a thick pulp. Pour into sterilised, hot jars and seal. Store for 1 month before using. Best consumed within 6 months.

MAKES 1.8 KG (4 LBS)

RIGHT: Ripe Tomato Chutney,
Green Tomato Chutney

GREEN TOMATO PICKLE

1.35 kg (3 lb) GREEN TOMATOES, QUARTERED
½ SMALL CABBAGE, COARSELY SHREDDED
1 CAULIFLOWER, SEPARATED INTO FLORETS
2 CUCUMBERS, DICED
450 g (1 lb) ONIONS, COARSELY CHOPPED
150-175 g (5-6 oz) SALT
5 ml (1 tsp) PEPPERCORNS
55 g (2 oz) DRY MUSTARD
1 litre (35 fl oz) MALT VINEGAR
225 g (8 oz) GRANULATED SUGAR
15 g (½ oz) TURMERIC

Layer the tomatoes, cabbage, cauliflower, cucumbers and onions in a basin with layers of salt in between. Cover, and leave to stand overnight.

Drain the vegetables. Tie the peppercorns in a muslin bag. Blend the mustard with 300 ml (10 fl oz) of the malt vinegar. Put the blended the mustard, vinegar, sugar, turmeric and peppercorns into a large pan. Tie the muslin bag firmly to the saucepan handle so that it is immersed in the liquid. Heat gently, stirring, until the sugar is dissolved, then bring to the boil. Boil for about 5 minutes. Add the vegetables and heat through without boiling. Remove the muslin bag. Pack the pickle into sterilised, hot jars and seal. Store for 1 month before using. Best consumed within 6 months.

MAKES APPROX. 4.1 KG (9 LBS)

QUICK TOMATO RELISH

15 ml (1 tbsp) OLIVE OIL
1 bunch SPRING ONIONS, CHOPPED
20 ml (4 tbsp) FLOUR
1 x 400 g (14 oz) CAN PEELED TOMATOES
10-15 ml (2-3 tsp) WORCESTERSHIRE SAUCE

Heat the oil and gently cook the spring onions for 5 minutes. Stir in the flour and cook for 1 minute. Drain the tomatoes, reserving the juice. Gradually stir in the juice. Finely chop the tomatoes and put in the pan. Bring to the boil, stirring. Stir in the Worcestershire sauce and season to taste. Cook for 1 minute. Cool, then chill. Serve with cold meats.

SERVES 6

TOP: Green Tomato Pickle
BOTTOM: Quick Tomato Relish

INDEX